IN TIME OF
CIVIL WAR

BERNARD SHARE

IN TIME OF CIVIL WAR

The conflict on the
Irish railways
1922–23

The Collins Press

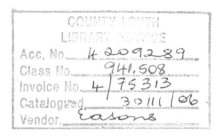
Published in 2006 by
The Collins Press,
West Link Park,
Doughcloyne,
Wilton,
Cork
© 2006 Bernard Share

Bernard Share asserts his moral right to be identified as author of this work

British Library Cataloguing in Publication Data

Share, Bernard
In time of civil war: the conflict on the Irish railways, 1922-23
1. Ireland. Army. Railway Protection and Maintenance Corps
2. Railroads – Ireland – History – 20th century
3. Ireland – History – Civil War, 1922-1923
I. Title
941.7'0822

ISBN-10: 1905172117
ISBN-13: 978-1905172115

Typesetting and design: Bill Bolger
Font: Scala, 12 point
Printed in Ireland by ColourBooks Ltd.

At the present moment I think we must admit – we all know it in our hearts at any rate – that the country is in a state of war, and the Government – whatever their reason might be – are taking over the railway companies – if they do take them over – because it is essential for the life of the country that the railway services should continue to run, so far as they are permitted to run at all, or else disaster overtakes the whole country. They are necessary to convey the National forces from one part of the country to another and to convey supplies to the National forces and to the people of this country in every corner of it that can be served by a railway.

Gerald Fitzgibbon, TD in the Dáil,
3 January 1923.

CONTENTS

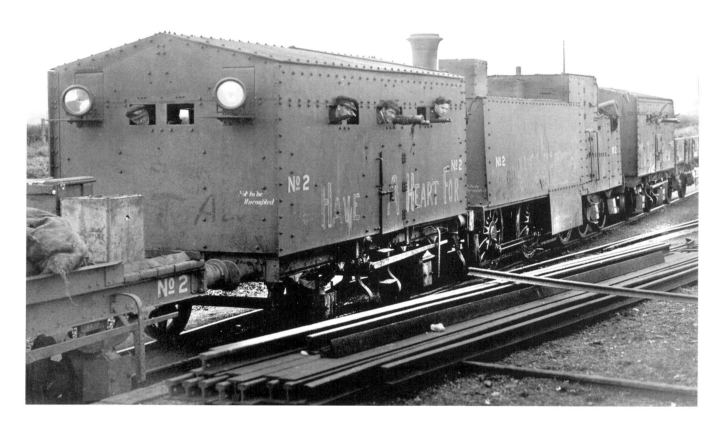

Armoured Train no. 2 at an unknown location. See page 100.

Illustrations are reproduced by kind permission of the following:

Iarnród Éireann. Nos. 1, 2 ,3, 4, 5, 10, 12, 13, 14, 15, 16, 29, 30, 33, 34, 49.
Military Archives. Nos. 11, 17, 18, 19, 25, 26, 27, 28, 31, 32, 48, 50, 66.
Irish Railway Record Society. Nos. 21, 22, 23, 24, 35, 36, 37, 38, 42, 44, 45, 46, 52, 57, 58, 60, 61, 62, 63, 64, 65. and page 144.

FOREWORD

THIS BOOK WAS BORN of the discovery, in the Inchicore Works of Iarnród Éireann, of a collection of glass photographic plates recording examples of the destruction suffered by the railway system in the course of the Civil War. On learning of the find, the then Chief Operating Officer – now Chief Executive – Dick Fearn is alleged to have made the unguarded remark, 'there's a book in this!' What follows is the result, though I must hasten to add that neither Mr Fearn nor Iarnród Éireann can in any way be held accountable for its content or for opinions expressed therein, for which I assume full responsibility.

With the passing of the 1920s generation and the consequent loosening of the taboo which restrained many from speaking or writing about this tragic period of internecine strife the literature of political and historical interpretation of its causes and consequences has assumed formidable proportions. It is in no way the intention of this book to enter upon this political debate, but essentially to record as objectively as possible the role played by the railways and the extent to which they suffered, in men, material and morale. Whilst the narrative aims to be comprehensive it is of necessity selective: a documentation of every single bridge blown, station robbed and train held up would both weary the reader and obscure the wider considerations which involved the fortunes and future of the railway companies in the new era of independent government and precipitated a fundamental change.

I must record my indebtedness to Iarnród Éireann and in particular to its Heritage Officer, Gregg Ryan, for material and moral support of the project; to Commandant Victor Laing and his colleagues at the Military Archives, Cathal Brugha Barracks, Dublin, for allowing me access to the relevant files and photographs and extending assistance beyond the call of duty; to Frances Sugrue of the Secretaries' department, Córas Iompair Éireann, Heuston Station, Dublin, for enduring my occupation of her office whilst lengthily researching the Company's invaluable archive; to Brendan Pender of the Irish Railway Record Society for his always generous advice and assistance and for readily making available photographs from the Society's collections. To these and many others, including my old friend and mentor Leslie Matson, I owe a deep debt of gratitude.

GLOSSARY & NOTES

The following definitions and explanations are directed, as will be apparent, at the general reader rather than the railway aficionado. In the course of the text technicalities have been kept to the minimum, but the inclusion of a minimal number is unavoidable in a study of this nature, particularly in the case of direct quotation from original sources.

Abbreviations The names of many of the railway companies of the period are frequently long and cumbersome; on the other hand the exclusive use of initials only is likely to irritate a reader not immediately able to identify CB&PR as against C&MDR or CB&SCR. A compromise policy has therefore been adopted of re-introducing the full name at intervals, in the hopes of refreshing the memory and avoiding continual reference to an explanatory listing. The excrescent 'Railway' has in general been omitted except in formal contexts.

Agent Virtually synonymous, with minor exceptions, with stationmaster.

Die-hard/Diehard A contemporary colloquial term for a militant Republican who took the anti-Treaty side.

Distance is expressed in kilometres except in an historical or verbatim context. Eight km equals 5 miles approximately. Track distances on Irish railways are still [2006] denoted in miles, measured from a terminus or branch line junction, with posts at quarter-mile intervals. Similarly trackside speed indications remain in miles per hour.

Down The railway term for a train originating at the main terminus of the line – i.e. the Dublin stations of Kingsbridge [Heuston], Broadstone, Harcourt Street or Amiens Street [Connolly]. Historically Dublin-Belfast trains were, and remain, 'down'. The reciprocal services are, obviously, *up* trains.

Fireman On steam locomotives, the second, and junior, member of the crew responsible for maintaining the fire and a number of other duties.

Gauge The Irish standard gauge (distance between the two tracks) was, and is, 1600mm or 5ft 3in.

Minor and light railways, such as the Cavan & Leitrim, the Co. Donegal and the West Clare, were, for economic reasons, built to the narrow gauge of 914 mm (3 ft.).

Injector A valve in the cab of a steam engine which enables the crew to inject cold water from the tender or tanks into the boiler to replenish the water level depleted by conversion into steam. Most steam engines were fitted with two injectors, one each on the driver's and fireman's side of the footplate.

Irregulars The term, in common use at the time by their opponents and many neutrals, applied to the armed forces of those taking the anti-Treaty side in the conflict. It is employed here for clarity and convenience and implies no political judgement. [The equivalent terms Executive, Republican and IRA appear in verbatim accounts].

Milesman A railway employee having responsibility for patrolling a given stretch of track in the interests of safe running (see 3 November 1922). Also known as a linesman.

Mixed train A train, common on the less-used and more remote lines, made up of both passenger accommodation and goods wagons. Having to shunt at intermediate stations, its progress was invariably leisurely.

Money At the time of the Civil War the monetary system, in common with Britain, was duodecimal: 12 pence (d.) to a shilling (s.), twenty shillings to a pound (£). No attempt has been made to express these values in present-day euros, but as a comparative guide a railwayman's basic wage at the time was 45s 6d (£2 5s. 6d) to 48s (£2 8s. 0d) for a 48-hour week (see 3 July 1922). For further, if irrevelant, comparison, W. & A. Gilbey & Co. were advertising a bottle of Redbreast 12-year-old J.J. Liqueur whiskey for 16s.

Names In the first flush of Independence many stations were renamed in Irish or identified bilingually. While some of these renamings have survived – Cobh, Dun Laoghaire, Muine Bheag, Port Laoighise (subsequently Port Laoise) for example – other such as An Uaimh (Navan), Rathluirc (Charleville), Brí Chulainn (Bray) have reverted to an English form. In this account names in verbatim records are reproduced as they appear, equivalents being supplied in cases of obscurity or ambiguity. Many politicians and others in authority at the time adopted the Irish forms of their names but, as in the case of the President of the Executive Council, W. T. Cosgrave, employed both Irish and English version [see 21 December 1922]. In verbatim transcriptions this variable practice has again been preserved.

Per. way/permanent way The entirety of the track or tracks on which trains run. The abbreviation is the common railway usage.

Pilotman In instances where normal signalling is not functioning, through sabotage or other causes, a train will carry a pilotman or **third man** on the footplate to act as observer. A **pilot engine** may in certain circumstances run ahead of the train to ensure that the line is clear.

Points The mechanical junction of two tracks, moveable blades permitting the 'making' of the road from one to the other. Points set against an oncoming train result almost inevitably in derailment and was a technique occasionally employed by those attackers with some railway knowledge (see 7 November 1922).

Regulator The accelerator or throttle on a steam locomotive in the form of a lever which when opened admits steam from the boiler into the cylinders causing the locomotive to move. The regulator, once thus opened, remains open, rendering any recourse to secure it in position supererogatory (see 26 July 1922). In this and other instances the attackers were clearly deficient in technical know-how.

Road The railwayman's term for the line of track upon which the train runs. To be 'given the road' is to be informed that the line is clear to proceed.

Section For safety reasons a line of railway is divided into sections controlled by a signal or signals and it is not permitted for two trains to occupy the same section at the same time, except in emergency or abnormal situations.

Slip carriage Several main-line trains of the period had carriages attached which, to avoid a multiplicity of stops, were 'slipped' or disconnected to provide a local service, braked and brought to a halt at an intermediate station, when they were taken in charge by a waiting locomotive. An example was, on the Great Southern & Western, the 18.15 from Kingsbridge which slipped a carriage at Sallins at 18.53 for the Tullow branch.

Special Any train not figuring in the current public timetable, run as a one-off working for sporting and other events and purposes.

Staff The procedure for working a single-line railway, of which there were many in 1922 Ireland was that a train could not enter a section [q.v.] unless the crew were in possession of a staff handed to them by an official. The staff was handed back to an official at the end of the single-line section, usually at a double-track station or passing loop, thus ensuring that only one train occupied the section at any given time. This practice remains as, for example, on the Waterford-Rosslare line, all single track with passing loops or stations. The 'staff' is normally exchanged when a train is in slow motion. Its release to a train entering the next section was, and is, controlled, by a staff instrument which releases it electrically on a signal being received that the line ahead is clear.

Time is expressed for clarity in the 24-hour system normal in transport timetabling, except in instances where the 12-hour clock has been retained in historical or verbatim contexts.

Upper case The literary style of officialdom at the time demanded capitalisation, at an almost Germanic level, of a high percentage of nouns, both common and proper. These have been retained in the context of direct quotation, otherwise adapted to modern usage.

Wheel arrangement Locomotives were, and are, identified by the number and arrangement of their wheels. The largest steam locomotives, virtually the sole motive power at this period, possessed three sets of wheels: a leading bogie, driving wheels, a trailing bogie. Smaller engines might boast driving wheels only, or a leading but no trailing bogie and vice-versa. Many railway systems, particularly those of mainland Europe, describe the wheel arrangement as viewed from one side of the engine – thus a locomotive with two pairs of wheels on the leading bogie, three pairs of driving wheels, and one pair of wheels on the trailing bogie was described as a 2-3-1. The Irish practice, however, was to look at the locomotive from both sides at once, so that a 2-3-1 became a 4-6-2 (a type, known as a Pacific, which, incidentally, never graced an Irish system). At the time of the Civil War 0-6-0 motive power was in very common use for both passenger and goods services. A 'T' after a wheel arrangement, as in 0-4-2T, indicated that the machine in question was a 'tank' engine – carrying its own water supply without recourse to a separate tender.

IRISH RAILWAYS IN 1922

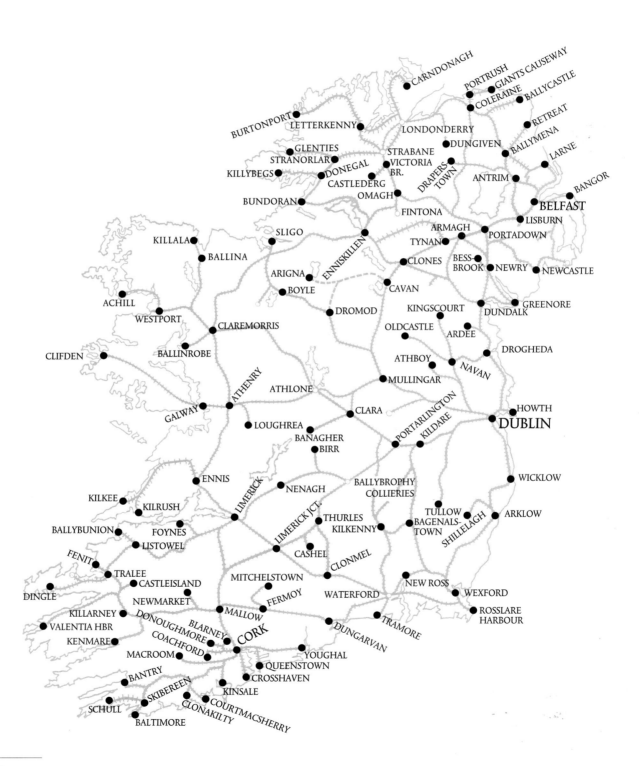

PROLOGUE

YOU COME ACROSS THEM, nowadays, in the most unexpected places – 'Railway Inns' and 'Railway Bars' sitting in an often decaying urban landscape from which all traces of the once omnipresent railway network have long since vanished. 'Station Roads' and 'Railway Streets' now lead to nothing more than a couple of once-proud cut stone buildings reduced to a disco or a distributor of fork handles, only the still-assertive architecture proclaiming the fiscal and social confidence the country once placed in a railway system that in its time served virtually every town and village worth talking about – and a not inconsiderable number which would scarcely have merited that attention.

Nearly every station, however big or small, boasted a cattle bank from which the animals would be loaded for transportation to the ports – most prominently Dublin and Belfast – and British dinner-tables. If cattle moved constantly in numbers, so did virtually every other commodity, home produced or imported: consumer requisites of all descriptions, agricultural machinery and produce, whiskey, shovels and racing pigeons. In the absence of any feasible alternative, everything was conveyed by rail, as were all those travellers who had not access to the novel and expensive automobile or were too poor or too remote even from the nearest railhead to have recourse to anything other than a horse or shanks's mare. Amongst all this traffic, material and human, the mails constituted a major element, as they had virtually since the inauguration of railways: special mail trains, rigidly timetabled according to the exacting requirements of the Post Office, taking precedence over virtually everything else. It was these trains, and their contents, that were to occupy the constant attentions of armed raiders in the course both of the War of Independence and the civil strife which followed. On 16 April 1920, for example, the down goods on the Cork Bandon & South Coast, carrying the mails, was held up at Kinsale Junction by armed and masked men who took away two Bandon letter bags, two Timoleague letter bags and one Courtmacsherry letter bag. In instances like these – and there were many – the information gained would more than likely serve to terminate the career of an informer, a police spy or anyone considered for any reason or none to be expendable.

To recall this vanished world of the early twentieth century in the context of a civil war is no mere exercise in nostalgia, still less a visitation of interest only to railway romantics. An understanding of the role played by the railway system in the months of the conflict is essential in grasping both its nature and conduct and the motivations and strategies of the opposing forces. It is equally necessary to comprehend the inordinate pressures put upon both those who directed the fortunes of the individual railway companies and the men and a few women, some 30,000 of them, who, for a nugatory return, were called upon to give unstintingly both of their time and their not infrequently divided loyalty.

Reviewing the publication *Irish Railways: Report of the Commission appointed by the Provisional Government, 1922* in the June 1923 issue of *Studies*, Fr Edward J. Coyne, SJ wrote: 'Forty six railway companies in a country of 32,000 sq. miles and 4,500,000 of people; and twenty-eight boards of directors controlling some 3,000 miles of railway line, almost one board to every hundred miles, are a sufficient *reductio ad absurdum* of the contention that there is much virtue in commercial management'. By no means all of these forty-six companies ran trains – a considerable proportion existed in name only, their identity buried in the complex history of the formation of the Irish railway network. Of the fully operational entities, ranging from the all-embracing Great Southern & Western to the unique and idiosyncratic Listowel & Ballybunion, built on a French monorail principle that nobody has since attempted to replicate, the names of their Chairmen place them identifiably within the social spectrum: H. J. B. Clements, DL [Deputy Lieutenant], Cavan & Leitrim; Joseph Pike, DL, Cork Bandon & South Coast; Rt. Hon. Sir Stanley Harrington, Cork Blackrock & Passage; D. McDowall Grosart, Dublin & Lucan Electric Railway; Sir Thomas Henry Grattan Esmonde, Dublin & South Eastern, former member of the Irish Parliamentary Party and future Senator; Rt. Hon. L. A. Waldron VC, Dublin United Tramways; John Fane Vernon, DL, Great Northern; Rt. Hon. Sir William J. Goulding, Bart., Great Southern & Western, whose co-directors included the Most Hon. The Marquess of Ormonde, the Rt. Hon Earl of Kenmare, Sir Henry Forde and the Rt Hon L. A. Waldron, the latter by no means alone in double-jobbing at this exalted level.

On this evidence it would not be unreasonable to assume that, when civil war entered its active phase in June 1922 with the shelling of the Four Courts, the control of the country's essential means of communication was very largely in the hands of men of Unionist adherence whose instinct, with respect to the two opposing factions, would be to call down a plague on both their houses. They were, however, businessmen as well as, in many instances, hereditary aristocrats, with the expectations of their shareholders to satisfy. Thus, once a viable national executive, the Provisional Government, had been established in January 1922 under the terms of the Anglo-Irish Treaty they were left with little choice but to create an effective working relationship with it and, with the onset of civil strife, to call upon its active assistance in maintaining a railway service that was seen by both sides as vital to the survival of the newly-born nation and the welfare of its citizens.

A European war followed by a war of independence followed by a civil war would be enough to unhinge most railway undertakings, and those of Ireland, with its scant population, perfunctory iFermoyndustries and Lilliputian companies struggling to show even a minimal profit, were more vulnerable than most. The outbreak of the 1914–18 war had seen 'the railroads of Great Britain' taken over on foot of an Order in Council which, however, made no reference to Ireland – then, of course, still under British hegemony. Known colloquially as Control, in the British case it involved financial guarantees and bonuses on wages whilst the Irish system, now carrying a high level of war traffic (between 5 and 21 August 1914 the Great Southern & Western ran 170 specials), was left to its own financial devices. It was not until, following the 1916 Rising, Irish railwaymen threatened a crippling strike that London acted. In August 1919 it established a British-based Ministry of Transport and the following month appointed H. G. Burgess as Director-General of Transport for Ireland, with absolute control of the railway system on the same lines as that operating in Britain, with a guarantee to the companies of net revenues as at 1913, a rise of seven shillings a week for the railwaymen and authority to compensate the companies for losses incurred while under government control.

While duly grateful for the promise of compensation (the GS&WR eventually received £1,043,000) the companies were already anticipating with no degree of enthusiasm the aftermath of the eventual ending of Control – the actual date was to be 21 August 1921 – unable, of course, to foresee that by this time the Irish political situation would have changed out of recognition. They anticipated correctly that they would be then faced with the prospect of continuing to pay the increased wages in a climate of no subsidy and falling profits. On 16 May 1921 the board of the Cork Blackrock & Passage complained that 'this Company in common with many others has been most seriously financially embarrassed by the increase of wages, and more particularly by the diminished hours of working [the eight–hour day having been introduced] and they find that if the subsidy is to be stopped in August next they will not be able to carry on the public service'. And the CB&P, which also ran a steamer service in Cork Harbour, had a particular cause of complaint: 'The Eight Hour Day has injured steamer traffic in a particularly disastrous way because the effect of it has been that the steamer cannot perform the circuit of the Harbour within 8 hours and they have, therefore been compelled to run a tri-weekly service instead of a daily service with the most disastrous results on their goods traffic, and as regards the passenger steamer service, the abolition of the [British] Government Dockyard at Haulbowline will very seriously affect the revenue from this source'.

Such concerns were being mirrored nationwide. In March 1920 Circular D.F.S/16 issued by the Director-General of Transport (Ireland) specified the rates of pay and conditions of service applicable to drivers, firemen and cleaners as from August 1919. This prompted the Midland Great Western to address a letter of protest to Sir Eric Golden, Minister of Transport, London: 'Owing to the less onerous and responsible work performed by Enginemen in Ireland as compared with similar duties in Great Britain and to the relatively lower standard of wages generally in this country, the extension of the Agreement recently made with the National Union of Railwaymen and the

Associated Society of Locomotive Engineers & Firemen to Ireland was not called for...' A notice addressed to the staff of the Cork Bandon & South Coast warned that 'Immediately following the decontrol of the Irish Railway Companies on August 14 [sic] it will be necessary to revise the conditions of service and rates of pay and salaries of all employees...from the first pay period'. For this company, as for others which followed the same course, the inevitable reaction was a series of crippling strikes: the CB&SCR cleaners, firelighters and coalmen came out on 26 August, followed on 13 October by all the men in the company's shops – the line closed completely at noon.

In a lengthy statement on the railways to Dáil Éireann on 3 January 1923 the Minister for Industry & Commerce, Joseph McGrath, summarised the situation then obtaining: 'Shortly after the ending of Control the question of wages and conditions of employment was referred to an Arbitration Tribunal set up by agreement between the companies and the trade unions, this tribunal being constituted of an equal number of representatives of the companies and the unions, with Mr Carrigan KC as chairman'. Awards were issued towards the end of 1921 but not accepted by the employees. The companies nevertheless prepared to put them into operation and a dispute arose which threatened a general stoppage in the middle of January 1922. The Provisional Government, which had just assumed responsibility, decided that under the conditions then existing in the country it was not in the public interest to allow the railways to stop running, and on 14 January an Order was issued suspending the operation of the Carrigan awards for a month, the Government undertaking to compensate the companies 'for any proved loss due to compliance with this order'. An agreement was reached between the companies and the unions to run for a period of six months commencing on 17 February 1922, later extended to 31 December. On 13 February the Government had announced that it intended to set up a Commission of Inquiry in the railway position, a move which was discussed by the chairmen, deputy chairmen and general managers of the four Dublin railway companies at a meeting in the Railway Clearing House in Kildare Street. The Commission began its enquiry in May and its findings were due to be published in December.

The railway companies had at the time equally serious problems to face as a direct consequence of political rather than economic challenges. With the War of Independence gaining momentum, on 20 February 1920 the British authorities had imposed a curfew from midnight to 05.00, with serious consequences for railway passenger operations. Not only was suburban traffic in Dublin, Cork and Belfast severely affected: train crews arriving at their destinations after curfew were not permitted to return home but had to find accommodation on railway premises, the majority of which could provide only minimal facilities. Somewhat ironically, the Midland Great Western had on 20 April 1920 decided to provide a bedroom and sittingroom for paying passengers at Mullingar station.

Another problem directly affecting the railways was of native origin: in the summer of 1920 Sinn Féin, in response to attacks on the Catholic population in Belfast, and in particular their expulsion from the shipyards, declared a boycott of goods emanating from that city. The move was sanctioned by the Dáil on 6 August and did not end officially until 24 January 1922. On 17 August 1921 W. H. McAdoo, the long-serving Traffic Manager of the Cavan & Leitrim, complained that the Northern boycott had cut off one considerable traffic – the commercial travellers (later to be elevated to 'sales representatives'). The ban was particularly hard on the Great Northern, which lost a great deal of its goods traffic, virtually every train arriving in Dundalk being examined and all goods burnt. It also had wagons destroyed in the course of rioting in Belfast.

There were those, however, who were not slow to take advantage of the situation. On 31 March 1922 four wagons, the property of the Midland & Northern Counties Committee, generally referred to as the NCC, and carrying potatoes and grass seed from Ballymena and Ballymoney, Co. Antrim to Charleville, Tralee and Cork, were intercepted on arrival at Limerick Junction. They were ordered by Irregulars to be taken to Tipperary station where petrol was sprayed on the wagons and their contents and set ablaze. The bags containing potatoes and grass seeds burst from the heat and a large quantity spilled out on to the permanent way, where they were picked up and removed by members of the large crowd which had assembled to watch the conflagration.

On 17 November 1920 the No. 1 train of the Cavan & Leitrim was held up at Mohill by the British military. Driver Hugh McGuinness and fireman Frank Mahaffy refused to work the train with elements of the military as passengers and were summarily dismissed. From that day until the end of the month six men, drivers, firemen and guards, were to suffer the same fate, instant dismissal being the lot of any railwayman who failed to observe instructions or the multitude of regulations governing his employment. On 7 July 1920 the 09.00 train on the Cork Bandon & South Coast was stranded at Bantry station, the driver, D. McCarthy, declining to work it owing to seven armed police being among the passengers. McCarthy, together with the fireman and guard and another crew, was dismissed from the company's service. A letter was subsequently received from the Cork Branch of the National Union of Railwaymen seeking their reinstatement on the grounds that they were 'acting in strict accordance with Board of Trade regulations', but the application was declined and it was decided to dismiss all the men who had been suspended and in future to dismiss any men 'refusing to perform their duty'.

If such dismissals caused severe hardship to the men thrown out of work, the effect on the railways themselves was almost equally drastic. In December 1920 the Dublin & South Eastern decided that 'owing to the continued depletion of staff from this trouble, the train service will have to be reduced, and in the case of the branch lines, completely suspended within a very short time'. In the previous August the General Manager, John Coghlan, had written to Sir Francis Dunnett, Secretary of the Ministry of Transport in London: 'the men, owing to fear of reprisals, such as have been already inflicted in many cases...will continue to refuse to carry military traffic; and as the Government is apparently unable to protect them, it is wrong to expose the Servants of the Company engaged in the working of the train service to the risk of life and limb, by calling on them to perform a duty which, however incumbent on them in normal times, is in existing circumstances impossible. My Directors feel that it is unfair to impose on them the responsibility of ordering their Servants to carry out duties which cannot be performed except at the risk of their lives. Further, any such order of the Directors would also jeopardise the Company's property, a responsibility which the Directors cannot accept unless adequate protection is afforded to it'. A meeting of the principal railway companies on 25 August decided 'that pending definite instructions from the Ministry of Transport men refusing to handle munitions would in future only be suspended; and that any trains held up in this way would be withdrawn and no further attempt made to run them'.

A further meeting on 9 September agreed that the Ministry of Transport must either accept the situation as it now stood or give the companies definite instructions to close any line or part of a line on which the staff refused to handle Government traffic. On Monday 11 October Sir William Goulding, Chairman of the Great Southern & Western, the country's largest railway, reported on a meeting of General Managers with the Minister of Transport in London. He told his colleagues that the deputation had been informed by the Minister 'that the present state of affairs could not be allowed to continue; that the Government were paying large sums to the Irish railways, the bulk of which was expended in paying wages to men who were refusing to do their ordinary duties. The Government proposed at once to tender generally munitions and armed men for transport by the Irish railways and they gave the companies two alternatives. Either they could dismiss their men on refusal to handle munitions or to work trains to carry armed men, and if and when the lines cased to be economically workable, the Ministry, in consultation with the Companies, would give an order for the closing of all or any of the sections which no longer paid their way in consequence of such refusal and dismissal, the Minister however would require the Companies to concur in this action, and to release them from liability under Section I Clause 8.1.13 in the Ministry of Transport Act 1919. The alternative was that the Government would introduce a bill to terminate the Agreement so far as the Irish railways are concerned'. The companies, left with little choice in the face of the thinly-veiled threat to their economic existence, decided to give the requested undertaking and to adopt the first of the two alternatives, signing an agreement to that effect on 12 October.

But that was far from being the end of the affair. Three days later the Ministry wrote to Sir William Goulding to the effect that the Government 'reserved to itself the right to deal with the railway situation in Ireland and the future application of such rights in any way which they or Parliament may deem necessary or fitting having regard to their circumstances existing from time to time'. On 10 November John Kerr, General Manager of the Cork Bandon & South Coast, told his board that he had been in Dublin the previous week and from information there received he anticipated that a gradual closing down of the Irish railways would probably be accelerated in the near future. On 9 December, the day before martial law was proclaimed in counties Cork, Kerry, Limerick and Tipperary, the Kinsale and Clonakilty sections of the CB&SCR were closed by order of the Ministry, and nine days later the entire Cavan & Leitrim railway was to suffer the same fate. These and many other closures, for longer or shorter periods, were rapidly rendering the railway system virtually inoperable.

The difficulties were compounded by a coal strike in Britain, the major, if not the sole, source of fuel for the Irish railway system at the time, which forced some of the smaller concerns to beg and borrow to keep the trains running. At the end of April 1921 the CB&SCR managed to obtain 100 tons of 'very good coal' from Murphy's brewery in Cork, and were negotiating with the Cork & Macroom for a further 100 tons. A quotation for American coal at 62s 6d a ton was accepted, but supplies from Belgium were deemed very unsatisfactory and could only be used when mixed with other coal: in the week ending 16 June this unhappy blend was the cause of five delays and one complete stoppage in the service. The previous month the shortage had reduced the schedule on the West Clare to one train a day. Looking back on the tribulations of 1921 the Rt. Hon. Sir Stanley Harrington, chairman of the Cork Blackrock & Passage, told his shareholders at their Annual General Meeting on 27 February 1922: 'We meet this year under very unusual and difficult conditions in the railway world...our traffic gross receipts for the year 1921 amounted to £35,304, against £43,327 in 1920. The decrease is due, amongst other causes, to the closing of the line by the military for a month in the summer, the cessation of the steamer service from the 15th of August 1921, the great coal strike in England and the Curfew and other restrictions on traffic'.

Dismissals continued as more and more men refused to work trains carrying British forces or armaments, but the consequent severe shortage of drivers, firemen and guards together with the hardship caused to them and their families forced the companies to reconsider: in January all those dismissed by the Dublin & South Eastern were reinstated 'on their signing a declaration to work all traffic' – a declaration in some instances more honoured in the breach. In this matter, however, the Great Northern, with strong Ulster links and sympathies, found itself in a somewhat different position, as was not infrequently the case. On 4 January 1921 its board received a deputation from members of its staff who had protested to the directors against the re-employment of men who had been dismissed for refusing to handle British government traffic. The chairman, John Fane Vernon, told them that if the men applied for re-employment they could not undertake to reject anything like all of them, but must use their discretion. He also pointed out that the Irish railways were under the control of the government, and that without its assistance the present high rates of wages could not be paid. The deputation then asked him whether the dismissed men would be re-employed in their former positions, over the heads of those who had been promoted to fill the vacancies: it was clear their concern was as much economic as political. Vernon assured them that 'the Company would not willingly take such a step'.

The dangers faced by both the railway employees and their passengers were tragically exemplified by the fate which overtook the CB&SCR 09.30 down train from Cork at Upton station on the 15 February 1921. It was fired on by armed men as it drew into the platform, the attack resulting in six passengers being killed outright and three wounded. Two of the company's staff, Richard Arthur, ticket checker and John Sisk, signalman, were seriously wounded. Neither man survived, Arthur dying of his wounds in the South Infirmary four days later.

The nature of the conflict resulted in the fact that records of such actions from an official perspective are far more common than IRA accounts; but in his autobiography *When Youth Was Mine* Jeremiah Murphy recalled his participation in a typical attack on British forces in Co. Kerry in 1921 in which the railway played a prominent role: 'Intelligence had reported a section of enemy troops would travel by train from Killarney to Kenmare on Monday March 21st. Their objective was primarily to deliver rations to the garrison at Kenmare. It was about twenty-eight miles by rail and this was considered a much safer route than the shorter distance by road through Moll's Gap...The route of the troops was through Headford Junction, where it was necessary to change trains for the branch line to Kenmare. They were due at Headford at 2.55 pm on the return trip. Two other trains were due there at 3.00 pm, going in the opposite direction on the main line. The plan was to ambush the troops when they had crossed the tracks to wait for the Killarney train. The platform ran along an embankment which rose about twenty feet high, affording good cover and a good view of the whole station. There was only five minutes to complete the job and leave the scene, before the two other trains – probably with large numbers of troops on board – would come into the station. Their arrival could be slowed by setting the distant signal against them. With these plans hurriedly agreed on, the column marched speedily towards Headford....When I was about two miles from Headford the firing started. It was rapid fire for about two minutes and then tapered off for another minute. I saw two of my pals, Tim Daly and Jack Murphy, running towards the station about a quarter of a mile away, so I ran in the same direction along the railway track. Very soon the train from Rathmore passed me by. I had hoped the other two fellows had orders to derail it. The sound of gunfire was still coming from the station. In a few seconds the incoming train would be there and the job was obviously not completed. Actually, the attack had failed. While the men were being assigned to their positions, the train from Kenmare entered the station a few minutes ahead of schedule...Our men had set the distant signal red [*recte* yellow] but the train, loaded with troops, continued on its way slowly, when they heard the firing. The casualties were twenty-four British soldiers killed, two IRA men killed, two civilians killed and five wounded.'

The partition of the country consequent upon the 1921 treaty with Britain was to create serious problems for the six railways which now found themselves operating on both sides of the border – the Great Northern, the County Donegal, the Londonderry & Lough Swilly, the Sligo Leitrim & Northern Counties, the Dundalk Newry & Greenore and the Great Northern. By the worse affected was the Great Northern, the Clones-Cavan line of which crossed and re-crossed the frontier four times within five miles. At each crossing passengers were obliged to submit to customs examination until, in the fullness of time, partial through-running was agreed. In the long term the economic disadvantage in which the companies found themselves as a result of partition was to prove fatal to their enterprise, but its effects were beginning to make themselves felt even before the Civil War began. Divided political and religious loyalties and the settling of personal scores under the guise of political action were exacerbated, if not created, by the division of the country, as the events in particular on the Cavan & Leitrim will illustrate. At Clones station on 11 February 1922 a bloody gun battle between the IRA and a party of 'A' Specials which had arrived by train from Newtownards en route to Enniskillen threatened a major confrontation between North and South.

For the railways, already struggling under these and other manifold difficulties, the Civil War was only the latest element in a chronicle of calamity; but it was to prove the turning-point for a system many of the minor concerns of which, with no prospect of ever attaining financial viability, were already struggling to maintain what in any event was no more than a token service. Many of these lines, in particular the narrow-gauge systems in the west and north-west, had been built under Baronial guarantee and were thus a constant and resented charge upon their communities. Road traffic was already a threat not only to these but even to the larger and more viable systems. But the railways were very substantial employers, providing not only 'a job for life' but, in the higher ranks at least, a degree of social status not offered by other employment at a similar economic level. And in return, railwaymen, particularly those directly involved in train operation, exhibited a loyalty to their employer often, in the context of the Civil War, at odds with their political convictions.

This loyalty, in the case of the driver, not infrequently amounted to a degree of affection for the steam locomotive under his charge almost incomprehensible in this era of the characterless diesel. The veteran Waterford driver, Jack O'Neill, has written of 'the uncanny relationship some men had with certain locos. Good work could be had from the worst of engines, provided they had the right crew for the job. There were drivers who treated engines like one of their own family and the loco seemed to respond to their kindness'. Thus the several instances of drivers in the Civil War period risking their lives when confronted by armed men by refusing point blank to assist in the wrecking of their engine. As George Hadden expressed it, 'the attitude towards the civil war of the railwaymen themselves was, with some notable exceptions, politically neutral. But it was marked by a loyalty to their profession that was often touching. It went far beyond self-interest. Dr [Peadar] Synnott says that it used to go to his heart to see tears in the eyes of drivers when he took over their engines to destroy them. "I verily believe", he says, "that they thought more of their old engines than of their wives"'.

There was also a strong sense of loyalty and solidarity amongst the railwaymen themselves, in spite of the conditions they were obliged to work under and the meagre rewards for such hazardous service. As the *Rules and Regulations* subscribed to by the principal companies expressed it: 'All persons employed by the Company must devote themselves exclusively to the Company's service; they must reside at whatever places may be appointed, attend at such hours as may be required, pay prompt obedience to all persons placed in authority over them, and conform to all the Rules and Regulations of the Company.' At the monthly meeting of the Waterford branch of the Associated Society of Locomotive Engineers & Firemen in December 1922 a vote of sympathy was passed with the relatives of their fellow workmen who had fallen victims of recent outrages in Co. Kerry. 'We emphatically condemn the wanton destruction carried out on railways', the resolution ran: 'And having regard to the onerous nature of the duties we are called on to perform, and are prepared to perform provided that we are remunerated to such an extent that we can keep our wives and families in some degree of comfort, and not merely try to exist on the half pay which we are now in receipt of, under the circumstances we are not prepared to take the risk involved by working trains after sunset from 6 February 1923. Whilst regretting any inconvenience caused to the public, we feel compelled to take this course in view of the treatment meted out to use by the company, who are out to economise our wages at this trying period.'

On 19 January 1923 the driver and fireman of a goods train in Kerry were scalded to death by the boiling water and steam from their derailed engine. And the War, on the railways as in the general conflict, took its toll of both sides. Four men were executed in Limerick jail for their part in railway destruction in the Tuam area. Railwaymen of both persuasions and neither were injured, arrested, imprisoned, dispossessed, dismissed. And as one service after another ceased to operate thousands were thrown out of their jobs; losing not only their livelihood, but, in the case of station houses burnt and razed, all their worldly goods. What follows is a record of destruction, attack and counter-attack, deprivation, injury and death no different in essence from that which characterised the conflict as a whole. In the case of the railways, however, it is also a record of a struggle, on the part of both management and workers, and in particular of the hastily-constituted Railway Protection, Repair & Maintenance Corps of the fledgling Free State Army, to keep the lines open, the wheels turning, the passengers accommodated, the cattle moving, the mail being delivered. It is also a record of the humanity and often bitter humour of the beleaguered operators and patrons of a transport network which touched in some way, as it never would again, the lives of a great proportion of the citizens of a nation in the bitter throes of birth.

THE WAR

SEVERAL ARMED LADIES

Saturday 1. The document transferring power from Britain to the Irish Free State is signed by Michael Collins and Winston Churchill. Carndonagh Barracks, Co. Donegal, is taken over by Irregulars. A Londonderry & Lough Swilly train is stopped at Newtoncunningham and copies of the *Derry Journal* removed and burnt. All goods taken by commandeered motor lorries to Glenveagh castle, headquarters of the Irregulars in North Donegal until the end of July. A Midland Great Western goods train is held up near Multyfarnham by masked and armed men who search 22 wagons for Belfast goods, some of which are destroyed. A quantity of bread is taken into Mullingar and divided among the poorer population.

Monday 3. When the 13.25 Cavan & Leitrim train from Ballinamore to Arigna arrives in Drumshambo the train crew and station officials are confronted by five armed men who order the enginemen to proceed with the train to Arigna. They do not allow the passengers, parcels or wagons containing goods for Drumshambo to be left there. On the arrival of the train at Arigna the raiders examine all parcels, etc., removing from the wagons two boxes of drapery; one parcel of boots; one bag of potatoes; one bag of rope; two bales of paper; 27 boxes of soap and two boxes of candles. [The Cavan & Leitrim, which opened in 1887 with a branch to the Arigna coalfields the following year, was one of the first light railways (914mm gauge) to be built under the Tramways Act of 1883. It connected with the Midland Great Western Line at Dromod, Co. Leitrim and the Great Northern at Belturbet, Co. Cavan. It closed in 1961 but the original Dromod station is now the headquarters of a heritage railway relaid on part of the former trackbed].

Tuesday 4. Snowfall in Dungarvan, Co. Waterford. Representatives of the Cork Bandon and South Coast Railway meet with Sir William Goulding, Chairman of the Great Southern and Western, to discuss possible amalgamation with that company. J. Coghlan, General Manager of the Dublin & South Eastern, arranges for a special train from Dublin to Wexford on Sunday next in connection with a pro-Treaty meeting at Wexford and on the 16 April for an anti-Treaty gathering at the same venue. He submits the relevant posters to his board, who request him to get in touch with the promoters of both meetings with a view to ensuring the protection of the company's property. M. F. Keogh, General Manager of the Midland Great Western, reports that the raiding of goods trains and stores together with the destruction of goods is a matter of nightly occurrence all over the railway – property of considerable value being destroyed or removed.

Senior Counsel's opinion is to be taken as to the best method of protecting the company's interests in the matter. The General Manager is to advertise that the company will not accept liability for losses. The Sligo Leitrim and Northern Counties, it is learned, is introducing monthly excursions from Sligo to Dublin via Enniskillen at approximately half the ordinary fare. Keogh is asked to arrange similar facilities from Sligo to Dublin via the MGWR. [The SL&NCR, opened from Sligo to Enniskillen via Manorhamilton between 1875 and 1882, closed completely in 1957 as a result of the severance by the Northern Ireland Government of its vital link with the main railway system at Enniskillen, much of its traffic consisting of cattle for shipment through Belfast].

Twelve armed men stop a train at Foxhall on the Derry to Burtonport line and take bales of bacon, a bag of sugar and two hampers of bread. They burn copies of the *Derry Journal* and leave a receipt: 'Taken by the I.R.A. signed O/C Foxhall'.

Wednesday 5. The guard's van of 14.30 Belfast-Dublin train is raided by armed men at Drogheda. They remove a parcel and two hampers containing racing pigeons, liberating the birds and burning the parcel and emptied hampers on the station premises.

Thursday 6. On the Londonderry & Lough Swilly the 08.00 from Derry is held up at Letterkenny by Eithne Coyle, described as 'an armed lady', who seizes and burns all the parcels of the *Sentinel* newspaper. Similar hold-ups by 'several armed ladies' result in the burning of the *Derry Standard* on the 14th, the *Derry Journal* on the 17th; *Freeman's Journal* on the 19th and the *Irish Daily Telegraph* on the 22nd. [The L&LS was originally built to the standard 5ft 3in (1600 mm) gauge in the early 1880s but was converted to narrow gauge (914 mm) in 1885, Though based in Derry its 160 km system largely served northern Donegal, extending as far as Burtonport and Carndonagh, though the route from Letterkenny to Burtonport was nominally owned by a separate company, the Letterkenny & Burtonport Extension Railway, opened in 1903. One of the most scenically spectacular lines in the country, it was worked by steam throughout its existence. It was replaced by road transport in 1953].

On the arrival of the 15.00 GNR train from Dublin at Cavan a party of armed civilians representing themselves as members of the IRA take possession of three boxes, the property of two civilian passengers who have travelled by the train. The lids of the boxes are forced open and a quantity of arms and ammunition seized. After the armed party leaves the station the two passengers take delivery of their three boxes minus the arms and ammunition.

John J. Rice, O/C Kerry No. 2 Brigade IRA [Irregulars] issues a 'PROCLAMATION – TO WHOM

IT MAY CONCERN. Warning is hereby given that from this date traders receiving goods from any person in the six county area will be liable to a fine of £100 and for a second or subsequent offence confiscation of property. All orders with firms in the six county area are to be cancelled and all goods on rail from such firms should be refused'.

Friday 7. Kenny's Advertising Agency, 65 Middle Abbey Street, Dublin, lists in a newspaper advertisement six firms 'NOT boycotted : David Brown & Son, Donaghmore, Tyrone – household soaps & candles; McClinton's Ltd., Donaghmore – Colleen Soap & toilet preparations; Urney Chocolates Ltd., Urney, Co. Tyrone – chocolates & Colleen Kisses, candy; Orelle Spice Co. Newry – Osco, Shuk & other poultry specialities, Ovo, Pomade etc; W & C Scott Ltd., Omagh – "Excelsior" flaked oatmeal; Newry Milling Co. – flour, grain & meal. The goods of any of these may be freely purchased in all parts of Ireland'.

Saturday 8. The goods warehouse at Ardee station, GNR, is raided by two armed men who take away half-a-dozen spades consigned from Messrs. Fisher & Co., Newry to Messrs. Hamill & Co., Ardee. When the stationmaster asks the men what authority they have for the action they reply that as the spades were from Newry they were taken away by Order of the Executive of the Irish Republican Army [Irregulars]. [The short branch to Ardee left the Dublin-Belfast line at Dromin Junction, north of Dunleer. It opened in 1896 and closed to all traffic in 1975]. On the arrival at Glaslough, Co. Monaghan, of the 05.30 goods train, Newry to Clones, Guard Retalic is arrested by a force of the IRA from the Glaslough barracks, to which place he is taken. He is accused of being a spy and carrying information over the Border, and is also charged with being a 'B' Special as well as an ex-British soldier. He denies the charges but is informed that he has been tried and found guilty. On being released he is told that he will be arrested again, and judgement passed on him.

In Co. Donegal the goods warehouse at Ballyshannon, terminus of the County Donegal Railways, is raided by armed men. A box of apples is broken open and two dozen removed. Four armed men hold up a train at Foxhall on the Letterkenny & Burtonport Extension Railway and burn newspapers. This train is again held up at Creeslough, Dunfanaghy and Dungloe.

Sunday 9. The Anti-Treaty IRA Executive [Irregulars] appoint a seven-man Army Council with Liam Lynch as Chief of Staff. Special trains are arranged from Dublin, Gorey and Waterford for the pro-Treaty demonstration at Peters Square, Wexford, at which the principal speakers are Gen. Michael Collins and Ald. Corish, TD, Mayor of Wexford. It is held to the accompaniment of a thunderstorm with hail and lightning. Only the Gorey train reaches its destination. The Dublin special leaves with a large complement at 09.45. At Woodenbridge rails have been removed and railwaymen attempting to repair the damage are held up by armed men who deprive them of their implements and throw them into the Avoca river. The telegraph wires are also cut at this point. The rails are eventually replaced and the train proceeds to Enniscorthy where, however, the driver is abducted and taken away in a motor, the train eventually reaching Wexford late in the evening. Of the two specials from Waterford, a GS&WR via Campile and a D&SER via New Ross, the former reaches Bridgetown to encounter rails torn up between here and Killinick. The damage is quickly remedied, but it is then discovered that the communication wires have been cut. The train is cancelled. The *Cork Examiner* reports the following day that 'this disruption of the line involved the holding up of the Rosslare to Cork Express boat train which was not able to proceed beyond Rosslare Strand Junction station. Here all the passengers had to pass the day in uncomfortable surroundings and with but very little accommodation. The railway authorities state that the train will not be able to resume its journey to Cork until 5 am [Monday]'. The driver of the Dublin & South Eastern special is arrested at New Ross and the train is unable to proceed further.

Monday 10. Two wagonloads of fire bars and brake blocks are destroyed at the Broadstone, Dublin works of the MGWR. They have arrived in two Great Northern wagons from Scotland via Belfast. Six armed men hold up the staff and, at gunpoint, make workers from the smithy smash the goods with sledge-hammers.

Tuesday 11. At Dunleer, Co. Louth, an attempt is made to hold up the 14.45 passenger train, Belfast to Dublin. Two armed raiders appear in the signal cabin and tell the signalman that they require the express to be stopped. Before the train reaches the station, however, the parish priest appears on the platform, and the men thereupon desist from their attempt.

Wednesday 12. Hampers of bread and two boxes of biscuits are taken at Foxhall on the Letterkenny & Burtonport Extension and newspapers burnt. The County Donegal Railways Joint Committee announces that 'in consequence of conditions prevailing in the County they cannot guarantee the running of any trains and will not be responsible for the loss or expense incurred owing to trains not reaching the scheduled destinations...'

Thursday 13. Irregulars under Rory O'Connor occupy the Four Courts, Kilmainham and buildings on the east side of O'Connell Street, Dublin, refusing to recognise the authority of the Provisional Government. The Board of the GS&WR is presented with a memorial from members of the clerical staff, arrested by the British forces, requesting the payment of their salaries during the period of detention. The company responds to the effect that it can pay no one absent without leave. There are reports of 'irregular travelling by parties of men or individuals belonging to Irregular troops'.

Friday 14. Good Friday. There is serious flooding in Cork.

Saturday 15. Armed men order John Delap to open his Goods store at Churchill on the Letterkenny & Burtonport Extension Railway. When he refuses they stop a train at Cabra but get nothing.

Sunday 16. Easter Sunday. Lady Gregory, friend and patron of the poet W. B. Yeats, is staying with her friend and colleague Horace Plunkett at Kilteragh, Foxrock, Co. Dublin. She writes in her diary: 'Just now the butler came to say there are no papers this morning, hears they were brought to Harcourt Street station, but burned there.' [Plunkett was an advocate of agricultural co-operation under the slogan 'Better farming, better business, better living'. Founder of the Irish Dominion League with the aim of keeping a united Ireland within the British Commonwealth, he became a member of the new Senate in 1922. His house, Kilteragh, was burned down on 29/30 January 1923].

Monday 17. The 17.25 GNR mixed train, Armagh to Castleblayney, is stopped at Kane's Rocks level crossing near Creaghanroe station by an armed raider who exhibits a red flag and closes the crossing gates across the line after imprisoning the gateman in his house. The engine with the passenger vehicles is uncoupled from the goods wagons and sent on to Castleblayney, whilst a number of wagons are sprinkled with petrol and they and their contents burned out.

Tuesday 18. Lady Gregory is returning to her home, Coole Park, Gort, Co. Galway: 'At the Broadstone [terminus for MGWR Galway trains] Frank met me to talk...at Athenry there was a boy stretched on a bench – to be moved into train. I asked Daly if it had been an accident; "It was a bomb – in Castlegar" was all he knew.'

Friday 21. On the West Clare, armed men remove the big-end brasses, cross-head spindles and connecting rod washers, together with the regulator handles, from four of the company's engines: nos. 11 & 6 at Ennis and nos. 1 & 4 at Kilrush, rendering them unworkable and leaving the railway with only two branch engines to operate the line. There is a rumour that the act was committed in view of the approaching Free State demonstration here. [The West Clare, immortalised by the surveyor, painter and humorist Percy French in the ballad 'Are you right there, Michael?', linked Ennis with Kilrush and Kilkee across a barren expanse of country exposed to the Atlantic gales which frequently disrupted railway operations. Opened between 1887 and 1892, this entire narrow-gauge system was closed in 1961. It has recently been partially restored as a heritage railway based at Moyasta Junction, where the lines to Kilrush and Kilkee parted. Of the locomotives referred to above, no. 11 was a 4-6-0T built in 1909 and named *Kilkee*; no. 6 an 0-6-2T of 1893 named *Saint Senan*; no. 1 an unnamed 0-6-0T built in 1887 and

no. 4, of the same wheel arrangement, built in 1887 and named *Bessborough*. No. 5, *Slieve Callan*, has been restored for operation on the heritage railway].

Saturday 22. At Headford, Co. Kerry, the stationmaster is held up by armed men at 12.15. They demand the keys of the crossing gates which they lock across the line. The 11.15 train, proceeding cautiously from Rathmore, draws up at the gates. On their way to a pro-Treaty meeting in Killarney, where it is a rainy market day, are General Michael Collins, C-in-C, accompanied, amongst others, by Seán Milroy, Patrick O'Keeffe, Fionán Lynch and Gen. Seán McEoin [aka McKeown], O/C, Western District Command. According to the *Cork Examiner* (25 April) 'it was well known that Mr Collins, Maj.-Gen. McKeown, Mr Lynch and Mr [Kevin] O'Higgins intended to travel by the down morning mail which connects with a train at Mallow, due to reach Killarney shortly before one o'clock. When this train did not reach the town at the scheduled time, all kinds of rumours were in circulation but it was not until some time afterwards that it was learned that an effort had been made at Headford Junction station to prevent its progress to Killarney...inquiries into the circumstances surrounding this occurrence went to show that when the train in which Mr Collins and his colleagues, and a good number of ordinary passengers, travelled reached the station mentioned it was found that some railway gates between Killarney and Headford Junction had been closed and padlocked with the object of holding up the train. Maj.-Gen. McKeown left the train and succeeded in smashing the padlocks, and the train then proceeded cautiously, eventually reaching Killarney over an hour after the scheduled time'. Armed men occupying the signal cabin refuse to allow the signalman to release the staff, which permits access to the next section of a single line, and Collins then directs the train to proceed, placing armed men on the engine. The only obstructions on the line are the gates at Minish crossing which are closed across the line and the train smashes the locks on these also. While the arrival of the train is awaited, some young men carrying rifles and revolvers and stated to be Irregulars loyal to the Executive recently set up at the Dublin Convention enter Killarney station, commandeer a ballast train and force the driver to drive it to the points at the junction of the Tralee line just outside the station. The track at Ballybrack on the Tralee line is also obstructed, though traffic returns to normal in the evening.

Following the robbery of cash from the Cork coaching depot, the GS&WR orders that all reports of robberies be sent in 'small paragraphs to the local newspapers, Dublin and English, and to the Provisional Government. The local IRA [Irregulars] are to be informed of the same under protest'. Men dismissed at Inchicore Works as a result of their participating in the Rising of 1916 are to be reinstated, though no men will be taken into the service without the usual medical examination.

Sunday 23. Michael Collins leaves Killarney by rail for Tralee without incident. Special trains arranged for his Tralee meeting from Kenmare, Castleisland, Dingle, Caherciveen and Newcastle West are all held up with exception of the train from Dingle which arrives on schedule in the morning. The train which leaves Tralee for Newcastle West to bring people from there to the meeting does not return as rails have been torn up at Barryroe, about 3 km from Tralee. Armed men prevent the driver from taking the Castleisland train out of that station.

Tuesday 25. An obstruction is placed on the line at Kennedy's Bank, between Corofin and Ennistymon on the West Clare. The 07.30 down is held up, mail bags opened and parcels taken.

Wednesday 26. On the arrival of the 12.20 ex Derry at Buncrana on the Londonderry & Lough Swilly an armed lady takes possession of all the Belfast papers. She joins the train for Carndonagh and throws the papers over the viaduct into the river at Messrs. Swann's mills. Ticket collector Campbell, who endeavours to prevent her entering the van, is threatened. On the West Clare the 16.30 from Ennis is held up by armed men between Lahinch and Milltown at Moypark and the goods van searched for Belfast goods. Nothing is taken.

According to a statement issued by the Provisional Government 'it was originally intended that the Commission of Enquiry into the Railways should be a joint one as between the Provisional Government and the Belfast Parliament but owing to the state of affairs in Belfast and the failure of the Belfast Parliament to carry out its agreement and undertaking, the Provisional Government has decided that it is quite useless to endeavour to act in co-operation with it. Consequently the Commission of Inquiry into the Railways has been directed to open in Dublin on Tuesday next'. The members of the Commission, chaired by Lord Justice O'Connor, are Thomas Johnson, J. O'Dea and Edward MacLysaght. The secretary is J. Ingram of the Ministry of Industry & Commerce.

Thursday 27. A number of armed men arrive in an armoured car at Porthall station on the GNR and endeavour to stop the 09.30 goods train from Enniskillen to Derry. The stationmaster and boy porter are held at revolver point, the latter being forced to put the signal against the train, but the driver does not stop and runs through the station. The incident is reported to the Official IRA [Free State] Authorities, who state that the raid was not authorised and was probably made by Republicans.

The Ministry of Transport, London, inform Mr Neale, General Manager, GS&WR, that the company's claim for the restoration of the double line between Athy and Carlow has been transferred to the Ministry of Economic Affairs, Provisional Government. A letter is to be sent insisting on payment of debts due by the British Government. [The line between Cherryville Junction, on the Cork main line south of Kildare, and Carlow was opened in August 1848 with double track. Athy-Carlow was singled in 1917 to provide track to serve Wolfhill collieries].

Friday 28. The 09.00 MGWR train ex Dublin (Broadstone) is raided at Leixlip station and £839 16s. 7d. taken from the clerk. The money was destined to pay the wages of staff at stations between Lucan and Killucan, Multyfarnham and from Inny Junction on the Cavan line.

Sunday 30. A West Clare Special from Kilrush in connection with a public meeting at Ennis can only proceed as far as Ennistymon owing to the line having been torn up at the eleventh milepost and the rails, with sleepers attached, thrown into the river.

West Clare 4-6-0T no. 1 *Kilrush*, built 1912. See 21 April above.

1&2
Barnagh, Co. Limerick.
See 6 March 1923.

3&4
Ballyvoile, Co. Wexford.
See 31 January 1923.
The train carried Mr Purdon,
District Superintendent and Mr
Capsey, Loco Superintendent,
Waterford, neither of whom was
injured.

6
A No. 3 DUTC tram at
Sandymount terminus.
See 30 June 1922.

7
Tram on the Dublin &
Blessington at Embankment.
See 1 July 1922.

8
Portarlington station, GS&WR, with Railway Protection Corps post on the platform.

9
Ballinamore station on the Cavan & Leitrim. The loco is no. 1, *Isabel*, built 1884. See 3 April 1922.

10
Ardfert, Co. Kerry.
See 18 January 1923.

11
Ardfert.

12
Ardfert.

13
Ardfert.

14
Rathcurby, Co. Kilkenny.
See 6 May 1923.

15
Rathcurby.

TICKETS IN IRISH ONLY

Monday 1. The 12.55 GNR goods train from Dundalk to Enniskillen is boarded by armed men who, identifying themselves as 'Free Staters', inform the guard that they are on the lookout for parties holding up trains. When the goods is subsequently stopped about 4 km from Inniskeen by armed raiders the Free State men in turn hold them up and capture a number of them. [Inniskeen was the junction for the branch to Carrickmacross, opened in 1886. It closed to passengers in 1947 and to all traffic in 1960].

Tuesday 2. The occupiers of the Coast Guard station, Bray, taken by force some weeks ago, are removing a bag of coal from Bray station each night. The D&SER board agrees to take no action at present, but decides 'that steps be taken to publish in the Press the various raids of the Company's premises and the losses sustained thereby'. At Coole, Lady Gregory writes: 'Mike, back from Gort, says the National Bank is now guarded by regular troops...No wonder, as the papers tell of Bank robberies everywhere, and of railways up in Tipperary...'

As a result of malicious damage to the GS&WR main line between Goolds Cross and Lisduff, Cork–Dublin trains are diverted via Charleville, Limerick and Nenagh, adding some 112 km to the journey.

Wednesday 3. In the past fortnight there has been a succession of raids on Midland Great Western hotels. At Recess a car was taken and not returned, the wheels and parts of a second car removed and 'refreshments' taken and not paid for. Lissoughter Lodge has been raided and some damage caused while damage to Inagh Lodge is considerable. Motor parts have been taken from Mallaranny. The Sligo excursion arrangements, having proved unsuccessful, have been withdrawn.

Thursday 4. The Limerick–Nenagh branch line which was being used as an alternative Dublin–Cork route is torn up between Shalee and Birdhill. The 08.15 from Cork is unable to get through.

Friday 5. The 07.30 train from Dublin is compelled to proceed from Thurles via Clonmel to Cork as the line between Dundrum (Co. Tipperary) and Limerick Junction remains unrepaired.

Saturday 6. At 03.30 the stationmaster at Dromin Junction, Co. Louth, is awakened and ordered out of his house by a number of armed and masked men who take him to the office and place him with his face to the wall, ordering him to hand over the key of the safe. He has no alternative but to obey, and the raiders secure and carry off cash to the amount of £6. 17s. 10d. Before leaving, the men state that they belong to the Executive Party [Irregulars].

Monday 8. The refreshment rooms at the GNR terminus at Amiens Street, Dublin are raided, the raiders departing with 13 bottles of Bushmills whiskey; 11 bottles of Coleraine whiskey and eight ounces of Gallaher's tobacco. They leave a printed receipt for the goods headed FOUR COURTS BARRACKS. DIRECTOR OF BOYCOTT and mention the fact that the commodities were boycotted goods [originating in the Six-County area] and that as such were being removed and confiscated.

Wednesday 10. The resumed sitting of the Railway Commission at Leinster House discusses, at the suggestion of J. T. Farrell, Secretary, Irish Railway Clerks' Association, the possibility of a central station for Dublin. The Customs House and Great Brunswick [Pearse] Street are proposed as possible sites, E. A. Neale, General Manager, GS&WR, expressing the view that the latter would cost 'millions'.

Thursday 11. John R. Kerr, General Manager of the Cork Bandon & South Coast, reports that two of the company's clerical staff left Ireland on the occasion of the recent murders in West Cork and that he has arranged to allow them to take their annual leave. (The shooting on 25 April of Commdt O'Neill, 3rd Cork Brigade, IRA [Irregulars] at the home of the Hornibrook family in Bandon led to the reprisal killing of ten Protestants).

In Belfast, a bomb in an attaché case is found on a Belfast Corporation tramcar in Ardoyne depot by Conductor Mansfield. It explodes without warning, causing him injuries from which he will later die. Two other conductors and a cash receiver sustain severe injuries. In an unrelated incident motorman Hawthorne is shot in the foot when his tram is passing the entrance to Butler Street in the Ardoyne district. Many such incidents and attacks are to be suffered by the Belfast tramway system in the course of 'the Troubles'.

Friday 12. The Great Southern & Western reaches agreement with Joseph Wharton on the provision of a motor service between Kenmare station and their hotel at Parknasilla. On the GNR, a light engine proceeding to Windsor, on the line between Queen's Quay and Central Junction, Belfast, with a pay clerk who is carrying £1000 to be paid in wages to the loco staff is held up by armed men who seize the money and make off in motor cars. On the West Clare the down Ennis–Kilrush train is held up near Ruan. A number of armed men jump on it from a nearby wood and shout to the driver to slow down. Mail parcels for Miltown Malbay are seized and carefully examined. The raiders take away the letter bag consigned to the same town, informing the guard that it will be returned in due course. They then order the driver to proceed after having been detained for 40 minutes. According to a press report 'this is the first raid of mail since the reign of terror' [That of the Black & Tans].

Sunday 14. The GS&WR runs special trains for the All-Ireland Hurling Final, Cork v. Dublin, from Cork, Mallow, Fermoy, Cobh and Youghal. Dublin win 4-9 to 1-3.

Monday 15. J. R. Bazin, Chief Mechanical Engineer of the Great Southern & Western, proposes the building of one 4-6-0 goods engine of a new type in place of the six ordered by Inchicore on 21 November 1921. In Belfast, a passenger's timely discovery prevents a bomb explosion on tramcar no. 231 at the tramway hub at Castle Junction, where it had arrived from Mount Pottinger. Passengers have disembarked when a man boarding the tram notices a quantity of smoke. He alerts the conductor, who discovers under a seat an attaché case containing a bomb with the fuse burning. Henry Smith, a flower-seller at the City Hall and an ex-soldier, promptly obtains a bucket of water in which he immerses the missile and extinguishes the fuse.

Tuesday 16. The General Manager of the D&SER reports that when a driver was abducted at New Ross, clerk O'Brien, goods clerk at that station, attended to the engine and filled up the boiler thus saving it from a possible explosion. He is formally thanked and awarded a cheque for £5. The same company is told that numerous applications are being made by season ticket holders for their names to be written on the tickets in the Irish language only, the compliance with which, it is suggested, will make it difficult for the ticket collectors to identify them. It is agreed to accede to the request in cases where 'special applications' are made.

Saturday 20. The railway bridge between Ballymena and Ballymoney on the Northern Counties Committee Derry line is blown up and no trains can get through to Belfast. Considerable damage is caused to several stations on the NCC. [The NCC, properly the Northern Counties Committee of the Midland Railway of England, was the successor to the indigenous Northern Counties Railway, which it took over in 1903. The line from Belfast to Ballymena was originally opened by the Belfast & Ballymena Railway in April 1848].

Tuesday 23. An application is submitted to the Great Northern for a subscription towards a fund for the maintenance of a North Louth temporary police force. It is agreed that if the enquiries which are to be made prove satisfactory a subscription will be forthcoming. Since March the company has lodged a total of 79 claims under the Malicious Injury Acts and since the 8th of this month there have been 19 cases of interference with the working of traffic.

A circular letter is issued to shareholders by R. H. Leslie, secretary of the Cork Bandon & South Coast Railway. 'I am instructed by my Directors', it reads, 'to inform you that they have entered into a Provisional Agreement, dated 4 April 1922, with the Directors of the Great Southern & Western Railway, subject to the approval of the shareholders of the two Companies under which the Great Southern & Western Rly. will acquire the undertaking of the Cork Bandon and South Coast Rly. from such date as may be agreed upon...'

Wednesday 24. The Northern Ireland Government decides to set up a commission of enquiry into the railways of Northern Ireland, chaired by Mr Justice Brown.

Monday 29. The Cavan & Leitrim saga continues. William McFarland informs his colleagues that 'about 4.50 am a motor car containing two armed men in uniform and one in plain clothes called to my house and awoke me. On answering them from my bedroom window the men said they wanted to see me and to come down for a few moments. I went down and spoke to the men who enquired my position on the Railway and on telling them they said I was the man they wanted and gave me five minutes to dress. I enquired what they wanted with me and they said the wanted to bring me for a motor trip down to Arigna. I was then obliged to dress and go with them. On arrival at Arigna an iron bar was placed in my hands and I was ordered to break in the doors of the waiting hall and Stationmaster's office. When this was done the men knocked up [James] Agnew and brought him on the scene and at the same time I was compelled to write a memorandum re-instating Agnew as Stationmaster. After this was done the men then threatened me if there was any interference with Agnew in his position that the whole British Army would not save me. The men then left.'

Drogheda papers report the death of Staff Capt. James Flanagan, of the Irregular force holding Millmount, in a shooting at Gormanston station. There are conflicting versions of the event, the Royal Irish Constabulary claiming that one of their lorries had been ambushed and stolen at Gormanston by armed Irregulars from Millmount who then set off towards Dublin. They in turn ambushed it as it returned from that direction and one man was killed. The Irregulars, in a subsequent statement to the papers, say that a party of officers from Millmount left Drogheda for Dublin at eight o'clock on Monday morning. Their car broke down at Gormanston, and they proceeded to the railway station to catch a train and continue their journey. At the station they were attacked and Capt. Flanagan was killed. He is, it is suggested, possibly the last IRA man to fall victim to the Black & Tans.

THE FOUR COURTS

Thursday 1. A mail bag is removed at Pettigoe from the 11.25 GNR train ex Bundoran by Free State troops for the purpose of censoring the contents. [The 57 km branch from Bundoran Junction, on the GNR Enniskillen-Omagh line, was opened in 1866 and in its time carried a considerable tourist traffic, catered for by a named train from Dublin, the Bundoran Express. The branch was closed in 1957].

On the Cavan & Leitrim, William McFarland's troubles continue. 'About 2.30 am', he told his board on 14 June, 'five armed men surrounded my house, three in front and two at the back, knocked me up and ordered me to dress at once. I enquired who they were and what they wanted, they told me they wanted me to go to Dromod with them and that I was to come at once or they would bring me. I again asked them what they wanted and they replied "We want you to re-instate Bridges as Stationmaster." I then dressed and went with the men who had a motor car waiting on the road behind the Station House. We proceeded by motor to Lough Rynn where the car stopped and three of the men went up to Rev. Mr Digges' house [J. G. Digges, MA, was a director of the C&L] and called on him to accompany them. I understood he refused to do so and the men broke in his door and brought him along with them, the car then proceeded to George Dobson's house, where he was knocked up and brought out and ordered to hand me over the keys of Dromod station. When this was done he was then called upon to sign a paper resigning his position as Stationmaster at Dromod and promising not to work there again. The car proceeded to Dromod station and the men knocked up Bridges and brought him out after which I was ordered to open the station doors, count the cash and hand over charge to Bridges. After this was done Mr Digges and myself were called upon to sign a paper recognising Bridges' reinstatement as Stationmaster and promising to assist him and also obtain for him his wages for the time he has been off work. The men told us that they were carrying out these reinstatements as reprisals for what was occurring to Catholics in Belfast and there would be others. They stated they were powerful enough to carry out anything they undertook to do. On Thursday night 1 June I was proceeding to Dublin, stopping overnight in Dromod so as to catch the early train the following morning and at about 2.40 am on Friday morning 2 June I was awakened by the proprietor of the house who told me some men were at the door enquiring for me. I opened my bedroom window and saw four men, one at least of whom was armed with a shot gun. On enquiring what was wanted they said they wanted to see me relating to Frank Kiernan and that I would have to sign some paper. They gave me a few minutes to dress and on going down and opening the door the men then called forward Frank Kiernan and I was told to write him an order reinstating him as from that day. I inquired whom the men represented and was told that was their business and that I had only to do as I was told. I had there and then to write the order'.

Friday 2. Lady Gregory is returning to Coole from Galway: 'there was on the platform at Galway a troop of young soldiers who marched to the train with their rifles and got in. There was cheering, and a song (I could not catch the air) and cheers to the very end of the platform. I asked one who was looking out of the carriage where they were going. "To the frontier." "What frontier?" "Belfast"! I said to Daly the porter as I changed for Gort [at Athenry] that these young fellows were pleasanter to look at than the Black & Tans and that I hoped there would be no fighting where they were going...he said a special train had come from Limerick filled with troops, who had joined the others and for the same destination.'

Saturday 3. At about 13.30 the British military block the line between Irvinestown and Kesh on the GNR in Co. Fermanagh by removing a rail and cutting all electric train staff, telegraph and telephone wires. The train service on the Bundoran branch is in consequence entirely suspended.

Bridges and Kiernan of the Cavan & Leitrim are arrested by Free State police and detained until 7 June, when they are brought up for trial at Carrick-on-Shannon, charged with intimidating William McFarland and compelling him to do certain illegal acts under force. 'But of course neither of them used any intimidation towards me', McFarland tells the Board on the 14th, 'and no court could sustain such a charge which was dismissed. Bridges has not since offered himself for duty.' Kiernan offers himself again on the morning of Thursday 8 and is warned off by a telegram to the officials at Dromod. 'On the intervention of some parties about Dromod', says McFarland, 'he left the premises and we have not been troubled with him since.'

Monday 5. An order is served on the Londonderry & Lough Swilly Co. by the County Commandant, [Northern Ireland] Special Constabulary, confirming the statement in the newspapers prohibiting the export of all commodities by rail from Derry to Co. Donegal. Special police hold up the 07.15 and 08.00 trains at Gallagh Road and remove all such traffic. The prohibition is short-lived.

Friday 9. Notice is given by Irregulars to the stationmaster at Burnfoot, on the Londonderry & Lough Swilly in Co. Donegal, that traffic will be allowed to pass to Londonderry but that trains would be searched for Belfast goods. George Dobson, stationmaster, Dromod, gets word that he may go back to his work there and takes up duty. The following morning he is warned by a man to clear out at once and that he had no business coming back to work there and that if he remains there would be no telling what might happen. Dobson again leaves Dromod. There is also a case of intimidation on the Thurles – Clonmel branch of the GS&WR.

Tuesday 13. The Bundoran Junction to Belleek section of the GNR is re-opened.

Friday 16. In the Free State area 620,000 votes are cast in the General Election, 239,193 to pro-Treaty candidates (58 seats); 133,864 anti-Treaty (36 seats) and 247,276 (34 seats) to Farmers, Labour and Independents, the majority pro-Treaty. Dublin University (TCD) returns four Unionists.

Saturday 17. During curfew hours three armed and masked men enter the engine shed of the NCC at Derry and order a worker who only took up his duties last Sunday to come out. They make him remove his boots, threaten him, and force him to run forward and backward on the railway track for some time with his arms above his head. They then oblige him to tramp through a bed of nettles in his bare feet and to climb a hill. He is then told not to go back to work and he walks off into the countryside, not returning to the city until after curfew. The outrage is apparently prompted by his having been given the job of another worker.

Monday 19. P. McTeague, late stationmaster at Arigna and who was appointed on 16 June to a similar position at Dromod as from today goes there to take over charge of the station. On arrival he is unable to find lodgings, all the houses in the village apparently having been warned not to let him in. He is obliged to sleep in the Police barracks and have his food supplied to him from Ballinamore. The GNR Board is told that the Provisional Government has taken over its Bundoran Hotel for the accommodation of refugees from the Belfast pogroms. The Secretary is to enquire as to the terms upon which the arrangement is to be carried out.

Wednesday 21. The longest day, but as dark and cold as winter. About 01.00 six GNR houses in Demesne Terrace, Dundalk occupied by guards Compton, Johnston, McAlister, foreman Robinson, signalman Moorehead and shunter Reilly are fired into. No-one is injured, but the occupants are ordered to leave Dundalk. All of them with the exception of McAlister and Reilly leave the following day and positions are found for them in the Six-County area.

Thursday 22. P. McTeague is approached by armed men and ordered to leave Dromod the following morning, his clerk, Jas. Flynn, at the same time receiving a warning notice to clear out.

The West Clare plans to run a steamer service from Limerick and/or Foynes to Cappa pier, combined with excursion fares from there to Kilkee. [A Mr W. E. Elton had acquired the paddle-steamer *The Mermaid*, built in 1891, for the proposed service but after a few trips she was requisitioned by the Free State government for troop-carrying purposes. In 1892 a special train, named 'The Steamer Express', had run non-stop from Cappa to Kilkee, at 13 km the longest such run on the West Clare].

Friday 23. The Deputy Chairman of the Cavan & Leitrim, R. H. Johnstone, orders that the line as between Dromod and Mohill be closed down as from this evening in consequence of the events involving P. McTeague. McTeague and Flynn leave Dromod, locking up the station behind them. As all the other available officials, and those who received similar warnings and threatening notices from time to time, refuse to go back to Dromod there is no alternative but to allow the station to remain closed.

In Dublin, Edward Addison Neale, General Manager, GS&WR, is giving evidence to the Railway Commission. Discussing rates of pay, he says that 'the railwaymen have gone to 45s 6d per week [for a 48-hour week] and to 48s in the towns classed as industrial. Drivers and firemen are paid the same rate whether their work is heavy or light. The driver of a branch train, where the engine pothers about to and from the junction, is paid the same rate as if he drove a heavy goods or main line passenger train. Guards are similarly paid: a man on a branch line, say the Killaloe branch, three and a half miles long, is paid the same wages as a guard on a heavy main line train. The Company contends that where the work, as at a small country station, is neither continuous nor arduous longer hours than eight should be worked by the station staff'.

Sunday 25. Commandant T. Carter, TD, calls to Ballinmore in the evening and informs the Acting Traffic Manager that he has received definite instructions from Dublin [the C&L offices are at 19-20 Fleet Street] to evict John Bridges from Dromod Station House, and that he called with Bridges this day and gave him until 6 o'clock tomorrow to clear out. The Commandant says that he proposes arresting P. McTeague, stationmaster, and clerk Flynn and putting them back into their positions at Dromod on Monday 26. The Acting Manager undertakes to consult with Mr Johnstone and to communicate the result to Commandant Carter as soon as possible in the morning. Johnstone agrees to the re-opening of the railway at once provided that Carter will undertake to provide ample protection for the officials and agree to leave the protection at Dromod until such time as things settle for as long as may be necessary. This decision is at once conveyed to Mr Carter and McTeague and clerk Flynn are arrested and conveyed to Dromod, Bridges at the same time being evicted from possession.

Monday 26. Dromod station re-opens in the evening and the train service between Dromod and Mohill is restored. Troops are now in occupation of the station house. On the GNR, four porters, O'Neill, Nesbitt, O'Donnell and Bradley, are kidnapped at Carrigans while travelling from Derry to Strabane to tranship traffic. [Strabane is the junction with the County Donegal and the Strabane & Letterkenny].

Tuesday 27. In Drogheda five Irregulars – Capt. Cooney, Christopher Burke, Martin Butterly, Peter Finglas and Divisional P.O. Costigan – are arrested at the railway station, the latter being quickly transferred to Dunboyne. They were attempting to raid a GNR train for Belfast goods and are detained in West Gate Barracks.

Wednesday 28. The commencement of the bombardment of the occupied Four Courts at 04.00 by Free State artillery formally starts the Civil War. The Irregulars arrested in Drogheda yesterday escape and five of the Free State army troops desert with the prisoners, taking with them nine rifles and a large quantity of ammunition. The situation in the town remains volatile. The Irregular South Dublin Brigade, which includes Wicklow units under Comndt. Andrew McDonnell and the mid-Kildare Brigade under Comndt Paddy Brennan, is ordered to concentrate in Blessington, Co. Wicklow, preparatory to moving on Dublin. At Raphoe, on the County Donegal, a wagonload of locomotive coal is taken away by armed men.

Thursday 29. At Buncrana, Co. Donegal, Free State troops take possession of the Londonderry & Lough Swilly station, commandeer a train and set off towards Clonmany and Carndonagh. In spite of strong opposition they overpower the Irregular garrison of Carndonagh police barracks.

There are no trains from Cork to Dublin, the 08.15, 11.45, 14.45 and 20.45 being cancelled as the lines between Limerick Junction and Dundrum and Limerick and Tipperary are torn up. The bridge between Limerick Junction and Emly is destroyed. All telegraph wires north of Kilmallock have been cut.

Friday 30. The Four Courts is abandoned by the Irregular forces and the Public Record Office blown up. The DUTC tram service is completely suspended on the North Side from early forenoon. On the South Side trams run on route 21 (Inchicore) from College Green but services on the Dalkey line (nos 6,7 and 8) and to Ringsend (1,2,3), Rathfarnham (16,17) and Palmerston Park (12) are maintained from Dawson Street corner. In the afternoon the Dalkey, Ringsend and Donnybrook (9,10) trams cannot get closer to the city centre than Merrion Square owing to shooting in ⬛

The British ⬛ ⬛ al & Liquidation Commission seeks offers for works carried out for the ⬛ ⬛ 914–18 war: The GS&WR specifies the crossover road at Queenstown [Co. ⬛ ⬛ (£40 offered) and sidings at the Ballast Pit, Newbridge, cost £826 (£150 offered).

ALMOST, IF NOT ALTOGETHER, AT BREAKING POINT

July
lúil
1922

Saturday 1. Most of the Irregular troops in Sligo have left and are beginning to cause havoc in the area, tearing up railway tracks at Collooney, an important junction boasting three separate stations serving Enniskillen, Limerick via Claremorris and Dublin via Mullingar. General McEoin, GOC Western Command, decides to return with his forces to his headquarters at Athlone.

A column of Irregulars from South Tipperary, soon to be joined by reinforcements from Dublin and Kildare, have occupied Blessington, Co. Wicklow. George Gibson, General Manager of the Dublin & Blessington Steam Tramway, reports to Kevin O'Higgins, Minister for Economic Affairs: 'A train left Poulaphouca for Terenure at 7.15 pm. On arrival at Embankment station at 8.30 pm this train was held there by armed men. A number of these men met a local train at Jobstown which would have returned from that station to Templeogue but these men compelled the driver to proceed to Embankment halt [where there are watering facilities for the steam locomotives]; on arrival there the passengers on the train from Poulaphouca were transferred to the local train and this was allowed to return to Terenure. The Poulaphouca train and crew were then made return to Crooksling and the train was there filled with Irregular Forces and the driver was ordered to proceed to Blessington, where the train arrived at 9.30 pm. The train and crew were held overnight in Blessington. At 6 o'clock am on the morning of 2 July the train was again loaded with Irregulars and the driver was ordered to proceed to Crooksling; on arrival there, the engine and crew were allowed to return to Terenure while the carriages on the train were held at Crooksling.' [The Dublin & Blessington, a roadside tramway running over 32 km of track including the Poulaphouca Extension, opened in 1888. It connected at its Terenure terminus with the Dublin United Tramway Co.'s system (route 15). There were no through passenger services but goods were conveyed between the two systems at night. The Dublin & Blessington was to close completely in 1932, victim of competing road transport].

Arly bridge, 3 km south of Drogheda, is blown up and up trains are halted at Dunleer and sent back to Belfast.

Sunday 2. Cork is the headquarters of the Irregular forces in Munster. A notice in the *Cork Examiner* states that 'The Editor of the "Examiner" and kindred publications desires his readers to understand that all matter appearing under the headings "Republican Army – Official Bulletin" and

"Republican Publicity Department" is not under his control, and he is not responsible for any statements appearing therein'. The *Examiner* is pro-Treaty. In the city, as night falls, a group of Irregulars demand admittance to the Cork Bandon & South Coast workshops and leave after two hours taking with them a small piece of plate iron. They are to return the following day with a written Order and commandeer some plate and round iron valued at £14.11s.8d. They remain on the premises until 05.00 the following morning, keeping 11 men employed cutting, drilling and turning. In Ballinamore, on the Cavan & Leitrim, the explosives store is broken into and 50 pounds of gelignite, 256 detonators and 20 coils of fuse stolen. Explosives are to be stored in future in the police barracks. The C&L Board is still agonising over the case of their three controversial employees, or ex-employees, and its 'Forcible Reinstatement' committee recommends that James Agnew be restored as stationmaster at Arigna as from Monday 19 June 'pending the report of the Railway Commission now sitting in Ireland, and that he be paid his salary from 29 May to 19 June 1922 as a temporary employee; Frank Kiernan to be appointed Porter at Dromod from 19 June pending the Report with a recommendation that he be appointed a head porter should such a vacancy occur and provided his services be considered satisfactory; John Bridges to become Assistant Store Clerk at Ballinamore pending the Report as soon as he can find two solvent sureties; Patrick McTeague, displaced Station Master at Arigna, be appointed Station Master at Dromod; George Dobson, late Station Master at Dromod, to be appointed clerk at Mohill'.

Dalkey and Killiney signal cabins south of Dublin are burnt out. All Dublin city tram services are suspended, as are all trains on the Dublin & Blessington line. In Donegal, the special excursion train to Kilmacrenan booked to leave Derry at 10.15 is held up for two hours waiting permission from Irregulars at Bridge End to pass through. They at first decline to allow the train to run at all but the General Manager of the Londonderry & Lough Swilly, Mr H. Hunt, goes to their position at Skeogh and after some negotiation satisfactory arrangements are agreed. A loco send from Derry to Buncrana on the orders of the Commandant of the Free State forces is held up at Bridge End by Irregulars and forced to return.

Monday 3. The Dublin & Blessington service resumes with a mixed train from Terenure for Blessington. This train is, however, held up outside Templeogue and a bag of sugar and 40 loaves of bread commandeered, after which it is allowed to proceed. On arrival at Blessington, another bag of sugar and two-and-a-half hampers of bread (comprising all the foodstuffs on board) is taken. The return train leaves Blessington at 09.35 for Terenure, carrying milk, an amount of which is taken at several stations on the journey, so than on arrival at Terenure only about half the quantity consigned remains. No further trains run. The MGWR has been notified that mines have been laid at Ballysodare bridge on the Sligo line.

Tuesday 4. In Drogheda, Free State forces commence the shelling of the body of 25 Irregulars occupying Millmount, site of the former Norman castle, latterly a British military barracks and now held by members of the Louth Brigade. They evacuate the position, and their post at the railway station. Six hours later a locomotive protected by sandbags and pulling one carriage makes a dash across the Boyne viaduct heading north. An armoured car opens fire on it with a machine gun, snipers joining in from the Cord cemetery. The carriage is riddled with bullets but it is not immediately known if there are casualties. The engine comes to a halt at Cartown Bridge, the Free State forces having taken up the rails, and its occupants escape across the fields.

Wednesday 5. Dublin city is now under the control of the Provisional Government but the Dublin United Tramway Company's headquarters at 9 Upper Sackville Street [now O'Connell Street.] on the corner of Cathedral Street has been completely destroyed, together with all the records and an irreplaceable photographic collection. The Victorian Gothic building had been acquired from Scottish Provincial Assurance in 1892, and the remaining ruins are subsequently demolished with the aid of wire ropes attached to a traction engine. The DUTC is currently operating some 330 passenger trams and a fleet of goods wagons over one of the most extensive and efficient urban systems in Europe. Following the destruction of the Four Courts, law sittings remove to King's Inns and the DUTC speedily reactivates a disused section of the former line from College Green to Drumcondra via Capel Street (route 27) to serve a contiguous stop on Henrietta Street.

Today the Dublin & Blessington operates two trains each way but carry no foodstuffs. On one journey from Blessington, Irregulars take control of a van on the train and carry goods from Blessington to Crooksling. The telephone at Embankment station is smashed and removed by armed men.

Lady Gregory is in Coole: 'Tim hears the railway between Ennis and Crusheen is torn up. No trains passing. No post...K.B. has been here, bringing strawberries for preserving... She says the railway bridge near Crusheen was blown up. And she heard a man in the signal box near Athenry had been shot and that Republicans had been in a train going to Galway, and Free Staters had stopped it and turned them out and got in, and went away in the Dublin direction. But she heard a train had come through to Athenry from Dublin. The telephone wires have been cut.'

In Donegal, some hundred Irregulars take over the school and RIC barracks at Letterkenny, later moving on to Glenveagh. Another fifty or so from Gaoth Dobhair, Crolly and Kincasslagh travel by train to Churchill, thence to Glenveagh. As tickets they produce notes signed 'Republican Intelligence Officer' on paper removed from the wireless station at Bun Beag.

Fighting in Skibbereen, Co. Cork. Services on the Cork Bandon & South Coast are maintained with delays but all passengers are searched on arrival at the town.

Thursday 6. The CB&SCR management decides to enquire whether the military authorities [Irregulars] are going to pay the men for the work they required to be done. The Financial Manager reports that in view of the state of affairs and of the fact that a consignment of motor oil has been commandeered from the company he has published a notice in the local press similar to that published by the GS&WR disclaiming liability for consignments. Owing to the disturbances at Skibbereen, he says, the traffic had been somewhat upset during the past week, the block wires having been cut several times at different places, but the train service has been maintained with fair regularity.

A special carrying a large number of recently-disembarked Irish-Americans leaves Cobh in the morning for Limerick. Owing to damage to the line it is delayed at Patrickswell until 13.30 when it proceeds in charge of a pilotman.

The Dublin & Blessington continues to suffer attack. A train leaves Terenure for Blessington at 14.00 but on arrival there is held up and the crew made bring three wagons to Slate Quarries Road, 3 km outside Blessington, where they are compelled to assist in derailing them and forming a barricade across the county road, after which they are directed back to Blessington and are obliged to remain there until 20.30 the next day, Friday.

'T. J. C.' writes in the *Irish Independent*: 'I arrived in Collooney from Manorhamilton in the forenoon of June 28th. On arrival at the MGW railway station I was informed that owing to a confrontation between National troops and Irregulars all train service to Dublin was suspended but that service was still maintained between Sligo and Athenry by the GS&W railway. I decided on going to Claremorris in the hope that I might get a train to Dublin the next day, but next day brought even worse tidings: trains suspended until further notice. The prospect of being marooned in the West of Ireland for the weekend or perhaps longer did not appeal to me so I tried to organise a party to go by car to Dublin.' After many vicissitudes 'T. J. C. ' eventually reaches the capital by road.

Friday 7. Lady Gregory writes: 'Christy coming this morning to do some painting says the signal box at Gort station was destroyed in the night and that all the railway porters have been given notice...'

Saturday 8. The first hot summer day for a long time. In Cork, one of the vessels belonging to the Cork Blackrock & Passage, the S S *Albert*, is commandeered by a party of armed men who take her to Blackrock with timber and stores. She is returned after two hours. [The vessel, a paddle steamer and the second of that name in the CB&P fleet, was built in 1881 in Belfast and continued to operate on the Cork Harbour routes until the service closed in 1925]. A train from Tuam carrying the Irish-American party runs to the site of an obstruction beyond Claremorris where it is met by another train which conveys the passengers to Collooney. Here, armed men in uniform take possession. A goods train which had reached Kiltimagh yesterday is returning to Sligo when it taken over by the same forces together with the driver and the guard.

Monday 10. General McEoin's troops from Boyle, under Col.-Comndt Alec McCabe, fight a sharp two-hour engagement with Irregulars occupying Ballymote who, from their strongly-held base at Collooney, are conducting raids in the area and derailing and looting trains on the lines from Boyle and Enniskillen to Sligo. A concerted Irregular campaign against the Dublin & South Eastern in Wexford is initiated with the blowing up of Bridge 399 near Killurin station. The 04.15 Wexford to Waterford goods is approaching with the signals indicating a clear road. Driven by Mick Conway with fireman Thomas Lee, the locomotive is 0-6-0 no. 17 *Wicklow*, built 1899. Both locomotive and tender somehow jump the gap blown in the rails. A breakdown gang arrives from Wexford at 07.30 and installs an emergency timber bridge, hauling the engine back onto the line, which by 10.30 is again open for traffic.

Eleven girls from the Churchill and Tearmann districts of Co. Donegal are taken to do the cooking for the Irregulars occupying Glenveagh. Cars arrive at Churchill station and take groceries off the train. Foodstuffs and clothing are similarly seized at Kilmacrennan and cocoa and condensed milk at Creeslough. The customary receipts are left.

Tuesday 11. A meeting of the board of the DUTC is held in a temporary venue at 39 Dame Street. Among those present are the Rt. Hon L. A. Waldron VC, Chairman; J. Mooney; W. Hewat and Dr W. Lombard Murphy (son of William Martin Murphy who was largely responsible for the development of the tramway system and the 1913 lockout of tramway workers). Also in attendance are G. Marshall Harris, General Manager; W. Lombard, Secretary; D. Brophy, Traffic Manager; T. E. Murray, Chief Accountant; V. F. O'Sullivan, Engineer and G. Collins, Law Agent. A letter is read from the Transport & General Workers' Union asking that employees be paid full wages for days on which they were unable to work owing to the recent 'disturbance'. The request is accepted on condition that they forfeit an equal number of holidays – or rest days in cases where holidays have already been taken. Another letter, from Capt. Keane, No 2 Brigade 2nd Eastern Division IRA [Free State], requests the company to keep open the employment of Michael Lee, stating that Volunteers are giving their services gratis and it is expected that employers will pay their full wages for the short period of their absence. This is also agreed under the same conditions.

The General Manager of the Dublin & South Eastern reads to his colleagues a diary he has prepared cataloguing the political disturbances since 28 June as they have affected the railway. Practically the full suburban train service has been run since that date except for two days on which the reduction was not considerable. He gives particulars of the steps he has taken for the immediate reconstruction of the signal cabins at Dalkey and Killiney, stating that the burning of these delayed the train service for only one hour. He has, he says, visited the scene of the bridge destroyed near Inch where he took steps to clear the obstruction and open the line for traffic. This was achieved within 24 hours of the damage occurring.

On the Great Northern, traffic is again interrupted by the destruction of two bridges between Drogheda and Dunleer. Passengers from Dublin are being taken as far as Drogheda and transferred to trains on the other side of the breach. Further damage has occurred on the GS&WR and the programme of trains announced to commence yesterday has had to be curtailed.

Wednesday 12. W.B. Yeats, visiting Lady Gregory at Coole, tells her he has not only heard but seen a train – an engine – with only one wagon, and only going as far as Tubber. She greets the information 'as the swallow that announces summer'. At Churchill, Co. Donegal, a train is raided by five ladies with rifles who clear it of goods which are taken to Glenveagh. Among the items removed are 30 large cases of tins of biscuits, boxes of tobacco, bottles of rum and bags of flour.

This morning for the first time in ten days a big mail consignment from Limerick reaches Dublin by rail. On Monday 300 bags of mail from Cork had arrived by the same route via Charleville. South of Charleville the train service is normal and it is now possible to get from Dublin to Cork via the Dublin & South Eastern through Waterford.

Thursday 13. In Cork, the Locomotive Engineer of the CB&SCR visits the Union Quay barracks in connection with the materials taken by the Irregulars but fails to see anyone in authority. He has, however, been informed that the Order that had been given at the time was all that was necessary. The Dublin office of the West Clare Railway at 39 Dame Street has had no communication from Ennis since Wednesday 28 June. It is not possible to reach the town either by telephone or telegram. In response to a general request for details of destructive incidents issued to the railway companies by J. Ingram, Ministry of Economic Affairs, D. McDowall Grosart, General Manager of the Dublin & Lucan Electric Railway Company, writes: 'A chara, am happy to inform you that we have not recently had any Raids, Activities, Seizures etc., but... on the 19th April 1922 at 1.10 am a party of 14 armed men on a motor lorry went into our Power Station at Fonthill, Lucan, and under threat of death forced our man in charge to open the Coal Store, from which they took from 3 to 4 tons of coal.' [The D&LER, a roadside tramway, opened from Parkgate Street as far as Chapelizod in June 1881, reaching Lucan two years later. Built to a 3ft gauge (914 mm) it was electrified and regauged to 3ft 6in in 1900. In 1925 it was again rebuilt to 5ft 3in (1600mm) gauge by the DUTC, operating from O'Connell Street to Chapelizod and Lucan as routes 25 and 26. It closed entirely on 12 April 1940].

Friday 14. In Waterford, at 08.00, Irregulars demolish bridge 457 some 4km out of the city on the New Ross line. [This had been opened from Waterford in 1904, connecting with the existing line from Macmine Junction on the Dublin Wicklow and Wexford system and encouraging that company to run a regular service, with restaurant car, from Dublin to Waterford. The Macmine–New Ross section was closed completely in 1963, but the Waterford–New Ross section remains in 2006, in place. It has seen no service of any kind for many years but local interests are pressing for its reinstatement].

In Athlone, General McEoin orders the entrainment of 120 troops for Dublin, departing at about 18.00, but at Mullingar he leaves the train with another officer and cuts the telegraph wires between that station and Sligo, shunting the train through the junction and onto the Sligo line. The party, no doubt disappointed not to have tasted the pleasures of the capital, arrives in the outskirts of Collooney at 06.00 the next morning.

The Cork Blackrock & Passage harbour fleet is again targeted by an armed party who board the S S *Rostellan* at Aghada Pier and order the men sleeping aboard ashore. Excavating work is then carried out on the pier. The men are ordered back at 04.00 and find nothing disturbed on the vessel. The *Rostellan*, a 95-ft. twin-screw steamer built in Belfast in 1891, is routinely employed on cargo services to and from the quays at Cork.

In a further reply to the Minister of Economic Affairs' request for information, H. Hunt, General Manager of the Londonderry & Lough Swilly, writes: 'I can only say that the events of the last month have practically killed the whole of the goods traffic on this line, and have prevented any developments of the passenger traffic, and its effects may be more clearly seen, when I tell you that, during the month of June, the working expenses of this line amounted to £7760, whilst receipts from all sources were only £4592...the difficulties have become so acute that my Directors are having a special meeting within a week to decide as to whether, under the circumstances now existing, it is possible for this Company to maintain its services. In an especial manner this Company has been subjected to raids, damage and loss of traffic practically speaking for the whole period of two years until we are now, almost, if not altogether, at breaking point.'

The GS&WR decides that it will be prepared to reinstate men joining the Provisional [Free State] Army.

Saturday 15. Conveyed from Ennis by military motor lorry and posted in Dublin, a letter reaches the offices of the West Clare from Mr P. P. Sullivan, manager's clerk, reporting that the Manager (his father) is seriously ill and is being attended by two doctors, and stating that for some days prior to the 14th only one train each way was run, that on the 14th the line was again torn up, and no trains will run on the 15th. All loco and traffic staffs were served with a week's notice on the 8th expiring on the 15th, and the agents have been instructed to make payments on account of wages out of the receipts to those who need them.

Sunday 16. Michael Collins, C-in-C, to Lt Gen. O'Connell, Curragh Camp Operations Area, 19.30: 'Your despatch of yesterday's date, which was not timed, to hand. You will note the following report received, check its accuracy and report the steps taken to deal with the possibility of a recurrence: BIRR: Barracks at Crinkle burned down by Irregulars Friday night, all roads blocked round locality and yesterday they occupied the three principal hotels in town. They took possession of Railway Station, and commandeered driver of train to reverse engine, and then they proceeded in direction of Roscrea. When they got about three miles out they broke up line and derailed engine and carriages. I think they are still in possession of the town.' [The line from Ballybrophy to Roscrea was opened in 1857 and reached Birr, then known as Parsonstown, the following year. All services on the Roscrea-Birr section ceased on 31 December 1963 and the track was lifted].

Tuesday 18. The request of DUTC men joining the Free State forces to have their employment kept open is granted on similar terms to those applied in the recent European war, namely that they be physically fit when they apply for reinstatement. There is a raid on Cork Bandon & South Coast's 03.45 goods at Drimoleague. A large consignment of groceries consigned to Lowney, Bere Island and two boxes for Sgt. Grey, Bere Island, are carried off. The wrought iron lattice girder bridge 367 carrying the D&SE New Ross extension line over the Enniscorthy–New Ross road near Palace is paralleled by a cross-girder bridge serving the GS&WR Bagenalstown [Muine Bheag] line. Both are demolished by explosion. Bridge 367, which is speedily restored, is to suffer demolition 13 times in the course of the ensuing months. The GS&WR structure will not be rebuilt for some considerable time. The GS&WR decides to close the Athlone-Portlarlington branch until the present conflict ceases and all the traffic staff have received notice dispensing with their services.

An engine is commandeered by two Free State officers at Bray, Co. Wicklow. The General

Manager of the D&SER is asked to make a special report to the Ministry of Defence. The possibility of the electrification of suburban lines is discussed [a step eventually taken in 1984]. Mr S. Byrne, Gorey, is seeking a subscription from that company towards the cost of maintaining the Civil Guard at the town which, he says, has been protecting the company's property since the outbreak of the present disturbances. Up to £10 is authorised.

Wednesday 19. The Free State Army assault on Irregular forces in Waterford under Pax Whelan, O/C Waterford Brigade, commences at 06.00. The attack is led by Colonel Prout, C-in-C. 2nd Southern Division and a former American cavalry officer, with 700 troops. Assisting him are Captains Paddy Paul and James McGrath, both natives of Waterford. McGrath, from Alphonsus Road, has been employed as a locomotive fireman on the Great Southern & Western and has been a member of the IRA since its foundation, as are the majority of his fellow workers. He has avoided arrest with the assistance of the foreman, Bill Finn, who transferred him to other depots. Prout positions an 18-pounder gun on the cliff over the railway station. With the arrival of the Free State troops on the heights all business stops in the city. All transport also ceases, the train crews having to shelter in the station for the duration of the siege since the railway bridge over the Suir on the Mallow line has been swung open, effectively cutting the Limerick line. For the four days of the conflict only the self-contained Waterford–Tramore railway continues to run normally. [The Waterford & Tramore, a 12 km standard gauge line opened in 1853, had no connection to any other railway system. It was closed, to great local dissatisfaction, in 1960].

Gen. Eoin O'Duffy, GOC South-Western Command, launches an attack on Irregular forces in Limerick. On the MGWR main line Engineer C. Seymour is carrying out repairs and is hopeful of a train reaching Athenry shortly [see 23 January 1923].

Thursday 20. In Waterford the 18-pounder gun is brought into position on the railway line to give covering fire to the infantry, enabling them to capture the post office and other prominent buildings. In another raid at Churchill station, Co. Donegal, two gangs of permanent way men are kidnapped by Irregulars. On the GNR the 06.00 Dublin–Belfast Goods is maliciously derailed near Clontarf in the Dublin suburbs. From Palace East, Co. Wexford, the D&SER agent reports: 'At 5.45 am this morning a motor arrived here with a load of armed men. Goods train arrived at 5.55 am. We were all held up by an armed guard – 4 of them opened all wagons, took all they required, loaded their car, and loaded one barrow load which motor returned for. They took flour, potatoes, sundries, tobacco and other articles, one chest tea and one bag maize. Raid lasted from 5.55 am until 7.20 am.'

Twelve armed men enter the Dublin & Blessington depot at Templeogue and having locked the three nightmen in a hut take an engine and coach and proceed at high speed towards Balrothery, where the loco jumps the tracks. They then return on foot towards Templeogue and remove two rails and some sleepers. The service remains suspended until Friday evening.

Friday 21. In the early morning the MGWR mail train is raided near Ballymote and mail bags seized and searched. The Irregulars employ the armoured car 'Ballinalee', captured from Free State forces, in the raid. It is the practice to endow both armoured cars and the Lancia rail-mounted cars with nicknames, 'The Customs House' featuring among the former and 'The Grey Ghost' (see 15 October 1922) among the latter.

Free State forces capture Castlerea, Co. Roscommon. A train conveys a large body of troops to within 3 km of the town where it is halted by a demolished bridge. A party of troops, on reaching the railway station, open fire on the signal cabin which is held by Irregulars, two of whom are captured.

Saturday 22. The Dublin & South Eastern announces the resumption of a full train schedule as shown in the current timetable, including the Waterford service.

Sunday 23. In Drogheda, a few of the Free State officers decide to attend a dance in nearby Bettystown on their night off. They miss the beginning of a gun battle at Drogheda station that lasts for almost five hours. The Irregulars begin the attack simultaneously from the viaduct and the Dublin road. Using a Thomson machine gun they strafe the station, the Free State forces returning fire as searchlights are employed to pinpoint their assailants. A lorry with a machine gun mounted on the back speeds down the Newfoundwell road and begins shooting at the men on the Boyne viaduct.

Eoin O'Duffy, GOC, South-Western Command to Michael Collins, C-in-C: 'The 3rd Seige [sic] of Limerick has been a success. History has repeated itself. First we had the artillery arriving by train at Nenagh...I do not think Sarsfield and his troops were as popular as the present victors.' [Patrick Sarsfield, subsequently Earl of Lucan, was the successful defender of Limerick in the siege of 1690].

A GS&WR ballast train arrives at Kildangan, south of Kildare, to restore a broken bridge. Two or three men armed with rifles and revolvers compel the driver to put up steam and move forward with the result that the loco and wagon fall to the road below, the driver having to jump to save his life. In the meantime the up train from Kilkenny has arrived at the other side of the broken bridge and a priest who is a passenger entreats the raiders to desist in their endeavours, but in vain.

Monday 24. At 16.30, with the Wexford Mail due to pass at speed, Philip Fox, stationmaster at Killurin on the D&SER, sees ten to a dozen armed men approaching him. They all run on past him except one, and he forces Fox to put the signals at danger and hand over the red warning flag. He then locks the stationmaster into his office and throws away the key. The raiders place the flag between the rails some 100 metres beyond the station. A train arrives from Wexford carrying, in addition to civilian passengers, 40 prisoners and their escort of 46 Free State troops. After passing through Killurin tunnel it slows to cross bridge 399, a temporary replacement structure, and, overriding the red flag, comes under fire from rising ground outside the station. The attack is concentrated on the first and third coaches carrying the escort party, which disembarks and returns fire. Lieut. P. Leonard, Escort Captain, orders the engine driver, John 'Sketch' White, to draw the train into the shelter of the station wall, but he claims that the brakes are jammed – he is later arrested for suspected collaboration with the raiders and responsibility for the deaths of three soldiers. The raiders, having failed to release the prisoners, withdraw after 25 minutes. The train proceeds to Enniscorthy, where White is taken off the engine and locked in with the other prisoners. Preceded by a pilot engine, 2-4-0 no. 25 *Glenart*, driven by Mike Hogan, White's substitute, Tom Sutton, brings the train, now running as a special reduced to the three military coaches, to the terminus at Harcourt Street, Dublin, where it again comes under attack from the tops of houses on the St Stephen's Green side of the station. In this instance the firing lasts only a few minutes and there are no fatalities, but about seven people including a boy and a girl on the platform, where some 300 onlookers have gathered, are wounded. The prisoners are detrained and taken in lorries to gaol. In the wake of this event the D&SER expresses concern at the failure to observe the proper safety procedures: 'the Military Authorities at Enniscorthy insisted on a pilot engine being run only 3 minutes before a Military Special that was proceeding from Enniscorthy to Harcourt Street, and the Station Master had to comply with the order, notwithstanding that it was in direct contravention of Block Signal Working Rules, inasmuch as it resulted in the pilot engine and the troop train being in the same signalling section simultaneously.' The General Manager is requested to inform the Government of this irregularity.

There is an armed attack on the Inchicore Works of the GS&WR. Three boys alleged to have been involved are dismissed, their fathers appealing unsuccessfully for leniency. The Portarlington–Athlone and Clara–Banagher lines are re-opened, but the road is again blocked between Tullamore and Geashill.

Monday 24. Clerical staff on the GS&WR are served with a month's notice owing to the disturbances in the south of the country. The wages staff are only working three days a week.

Tuesday 25. The remains of Corporal McMahon, 7 Arran Quay, Dublin and Volunteer M. Quirk, victims of Monday's ambush at Killurin, are removed from the Wexford County Home Hospital to the Cathedral, Enniscorthy, escorted by a contingent of Free State troops, They are later brought to Dublin by train.

Wednesday 26. The GNR 06.00 Dublin–Belfast goods is derailed approaching Howth Junction. Twenty to thirty armed men appear ahead of the train and call on the driver to stop. On his failing to obey promptly they open fire on the train crew who, however, escape injury. The train is brought to a standstill and the driver, fireman and guard compelled to leave the engine and run. Armed men mount the footplate and open the regulator, tying it back with wire and putting the loco in motion at high speed. It and its train hit the gap in the permanent way, derailing the engine and several wagons and blocking both up and down lines. Traffic is, nevertheless, able to resume by 15.00.

Thursday 27. At Coole, Lady Gregory writes: 'Some newspapers this morning up to Saturday 22nd were brought by a railway wagon coming from Athenry to see if the line is clear.'

Friday 28. 'Although so far as transport is concerned Rosslare Harbour is at a standstill', says the *Waterford News*, 'the railway company are displaying the anxiety they feel for their employees by distributing the tidying up work, etc. amongst the whole of them. Every man who was suspended has got half time work up to the present, but the chances are that even this will not be continued.' The new Great Southern & Western hotel at Killarney is occupied by Irregular forces.

Saturday 29. In the month since 27 June the GS&WR has suffered disruption of the per. way in 113 places; 37 bridges carrying the railway and 23 overbridges destroyed; 16 signal cabins destroyed or damaged; two other buildings burnt and three engines derailed. On the West Clare a bridge near Miltown Malbay is destroyed, cutting the connection between Ennis and Kilrush which is the principal supply route for south Clare. Flour is selling at 35s 6d per half sack and other foodstuffs are scarce.

Monday 31. At Mountcharles, on the County Donegal line to Killybegs, porter Woodcock is held up and robbed of £19 16s which he has collected locally in freight payments.

Tuesday 1. Cold and showery in the West. Lady Gregory is told that Kiltartan bridge, on the Ennis-Athenry line north of Gort, has been blown up the previous night. 'The train that was coming was signalled to go back, and we are more than ever cut away...' The Dublin & South Eastern decides to grant £1 each to two members of the Gorey staff who rode to Arklow on bicycles during the night to convey the information that bridge no. 280 at milepost 59 had been broken. It is also agreed that, having regard to the state of the country and the urgent necessity to give every possible assistance to the Provisional Government, the company will do everything possible to continue the present rates of wages and conditions of service to the end of the year out of their own resources. The chairman, Sir Thomas Grattan Esmonde, observes that 'the principal reason for the weakening of the cash position is the failure of the Station receipts to come up to expectation since the third week in June, owing to the trouble throughout the country. For the past six weeks the receipts have fallen below expectation to the amount of about £2500 per week'. An unsuccessful attempt is made to destroy Dunbrody bridge over the Arthurstown-New Ross road in Co Wexford – a second attempt, equally unsuccessful, is made on the 19th.

Wednesday 2. Denis Sheehy is employed by the Tralee and Fenit Railway Company at Fenit harbour station. He is looking through a window of the office and sees the steamer *Lady Wicklow* coming into port. Built in 1895 for the Dublin–Liverpool service and originally named plain *Wicklow*, she was taken over from the City of Dublin Steam Packet Co. by the British & Irish Steam Packet Co (B&I) in 1919 and the name changed. Today the tide is unsuitable and the pilot has great difficulty bringing her alongside. Once the *Lady Wicklow* is moored the Vickers gun mounted on the armoured car carried on board, together with Lewis guns and rifles, open up from the deck, the Vickers gunners targeting the upper gable end of the coastguard station. This cover fire enables the disembarking troops to advance along the pier towards the village. The leading units move forward along the exposed straight and narrow pier towards what are expected to be the defensive positions of the Irregulars, with the ever-present danger of exploding mines. Fortunately for the attackers there is no explosion and railway wagons on the pier afford protection, the troops taking cover behind them and pushing them almost as far as the station. From there they advance, opening fire on selected targets. [The Tralee & Fenit Railway Company opened the line in 1887. It was taken over by the GS&WR in 1901, but the name lingered on in popular parlance. It closed to passengers, apart from occasional excursions, in 1934 and to all traffic in 1978. Subsequent attempts by a preservation group to reinstate it came to nothing. Niall Harrington, in *Kerry Landing* (1992) recalled: 'I have happy memories of travelling with my boyhood friends on the mid-week and Sunday excursion trains run by the Tralee and Fenit Railway Company from Tralee to Fenit, with intervening stops at the Spa and Kilfenora. On fine days, the trains carried capacity crowds out for a day's enjoyment at that delightful spot'].

The Free State forces advance on Tralee, where there is fierce fighting before the town is taken. Batt Dowling, Capt. of the Ballyroe Company of the Irregulars, later remembers that the mines used for their demolishing of road bridges were made in Ballymullen barracks by Jimmy Daly of Killarney, a fitter employed by the Tralee and Dingle Railway Company. 'The Staters were entering the town by the time the mines were delivered to the Ballyroe Company', he said, 'entirely too late for us to make effective use of them that day, and a pointer to the fact that the landing at Fenit had taken everybody by surprise. We did use some of the mines on subsequent days to blow up a section of the Fenit railway line, the railway bridge on the North Kerry line at Tubrid, and the bridge near Callaghan's of Ballyroe.'

Thursday 3. The anti-Treaty North-Eastern Command [Irregulars] in a statement warns the Irish Engineering Union: 'Owing to the use of railways by the "Free State" Headquarters for the conveyance of troops and war material for the purposes of Army communication, the destruction of railways under "Free State" control is an essential part of our military policy. Unless absolutely essential we are reluctant to interfere with those services which are a convenience to the civil population. This decision has, however, been forced upon us by reason of the fact that the chief work of the railways at present is army work; that the railway authorities give allegiance to the so-called Provisional Government, and that organised Labour has, up to the present, freely co-operated in assisting the "Free State" and the British Government in their attempt to exterminate the Republican forces.'

John F. Sides, Chief Engineer, GS&WR, writes to Kevin O'Higgins, Minister of Economic Affairs: 'The Company's stock of permanent way tools has been very seriously depleted within the past few months owing to continual raids, and I would point out that requisitioning these tools may lead to delay in carrying out the necessary repairs to the railway. I am informed that all telegraph wires were cut at the 4¼ mile post Ennis branch on 15th ult. by Free State Troops.'

Friday 4. At Ballyvoile, Co. Waterford, the road and rail bridges across the river Dalligan are blown up, the explosions being heard for a considerable distance. The railway viaduct, according to the *Waterford News*, 'rose to a great height, perhaps 100 feet, supported on masonry pillars, and was a source of uneasiness to timid people to cross it in the railway. As a consequence of this destruction the train cannot run from Dungarvan to Durrow'. [See 17 August below and 31 January 1923].

Saturday 5. A letter from Ernie O'Malley's Irregular headquarters in Dublin threatens to shoot railway and other public service workers for carrying out their duties, which he construes as collaborating with the Provisional Government. The letter is read out and those responsible for it are denounced by E. P. Hart of the Amalgamated Transport and General Workers' Union at the Annual Conference of the Irish Labour Party and Trades Union Council, which opens in Dublin two days later. [Earnán (Ernie) O'Malley, a veteran of the War of Independence, took the Republican (Irregular) side and on 10 July 1922 had been appointed Assistant Chief of Staff by Liam Lynch]. A plan by the Irregulars to isolate Dublin by severing communications and blowing bridges, scheduled for today, has been forestalled by the capture of their battle plans by Col. Hugo McNeill.

In Kerry, Jeremiah Murphy is handed a dispatch: 'To O/C 5th Battalion H.Q. Destroy all available bridges. Evacuate the [Rathmore] barracks and destroy same at your discretion. From O/C. Kerry no. 2 Brigade' [John Joe Rice]. Murphy later recalled that 'it was obvious that we couldn't hold the barracks and do the job on the bridges also, so we called in some more men. After securing a hand car from the railway station nearby, we set out for the west towards Killarney along the railway tracks. Our tools and supplies rode on the car and we pushed it west of Headford station. There were no bridges of importance further on, and we had no knowledge of the advance of the enemy. No trains had run since Tralee was occupied about a week before. We burned a few bridges, wrecked the signal equipment at the station, and removed some rails at a bend. The idea was to make everything as difficult as possible to replace. We built a large fire of railway sleepers and piled a lot of rails on top to be bent by the heat. My colleagues wanted to burn the Quagmire bridge [near Kilquane], but I reasoned it could not be destroyed, as it did not contain enough wood. While throwing some rails off this rather high structure into the river, a few of us almost got our skulls smashed by a teetering rail. At Barraduff bridge we knocked out another span'.

A proclamation issued by Gen. O'Duffy, O/C, Eastern District Command, states that troops are authorised to fire on persons committing a number of offences including destroying bridges and railway lines.

Sunday 6. At a meeting of the Ballybrophy branch of the National Union of Railwaymen, William McEvoy, presiding a resolution is passed unanimously stating that 'this branch of Irish railwaymen whose members in the past took a prominent part in the fight for the country's emancipation strongly condemn the policy of destruction adopted by the Irregular forces. The burning of our old and historic buildings, the destruction of railways, signal cabins etc., the dislocation of all industries that are the wealth of the people will not, in our opinion, obtain freedom for our country...'

Monday 7. The S S *Arvonia*, commandeered by General Emmet Dalton from the London & North Western Railway's Holyhead–Dublin service, sails with 500 men for Cork with the *Lady Wicklow*. The *Arvonia*, 2642 tons, was built in 1897 as the *Cambria* and renamed in 1920. An official release from GHQ Army Publicity states that 'from information which came to hand from various sources it was learned that preparations were being made by Irregulars to bring off a coup in the Dublin area on Saturday night. Numbers of Irregulars came to Dublin from Cork, travelling via Liverpool, in order to take part in the proposed operations. The chief objective of the Irregulars was to isolate Dublin by destroying the bridges, road, railways and other means of communication'. The plan was frustrated and 160 prisoners taken.

On the West Clare the 09.00 up train is carrying the remains of a Free State officer for burial at Miltown. The line is torn up at a bridge near Craggaknock, and the telephone wires cut. At Geashill on the Tullamore–Athlone branch of the GS&WR a large body of Irregulars arrives as a special train is passing. They hold it up but discover that it consists entirely of empty wagons.

Tuesday 8. Dungarvan is evacuated by Irregular forces. The Cork no. 1 Brigade, under Mick Murphy, who have constituted the main portion of the garrison, leave the town by two trains which they seize at the station. When they have passed Cappoquin a further party of Irregulars, arriving by motor car, blow up the rail and road bridges. Free State troops are landed at Passage, Co. Cork, taking the Irregular forces by surprise and meeting with little resistance, except at Rochestown and Douglas from Mick Murphy, returning from Waterford.

On the Cork Bandon & South Coast, Millscannig Bridge is damaged by explosives and traffic can only be worked as far as Ballineen. The Great Island bridges on the GS&WR Cork–Cobh line are destroyed, preventing the running of the Dublin–Cork–Cobh Day Mail: it is never again to run beyond Cork. Landings also take place at Youghal and Union Hall. On the D&SER the General Manager is given authority to endeavour to re-arrange the goods train service so that it may be run during the hours of daylight, 'as a measure of safety during the unsettled state of the country'.

Wednesday 9. The Mallow viaduct, carrying the Dublin–Cork main line of the GS&WR across the river Blackwater, is completely destroyed by explosives, three of the ten masonry arches being blown up and the rest subsequently collapsing into the river. With Cork effectively cut off by rail from the rest of the country a temporary station, 'Mallow South', is established within days on the southern bank of the river. The playwright and Abbey Theatre director Lennox Robinson describes in his autobiography *Three Homes* (1938) how he 'left Cork by the 10.15 on Monday morning, but were a little late in starting as an armoured train was ahead of us. At Mallow we had to leave the train and get across the town in cars as of course the bridge had been blown up.

The line all the way to Dublin is strongly held with troops and all through County Cork there are frequent guard posts at bridges, etc., beyond that the soldiers are mostly concentrated at the stations which are all sand-bagged and some wired as well. We had rather an unpleasant ten minutes the night before I left Ballymoney when an attack was made on the railway bridge...' Erskine Childers, who will be described by *The Irish Times* on 6 September as 'the chief military brain amongst the Irregulars', is blamed for the destruction of the Mallow Viaduct. 'For some strange reason', wrote Calton Younger, 'poor Childers, who was no more than a propagandist, 'was held responsible for every railway torn up and every bridge destroyed'. The Cork-born journalist Lionel Fleming writes in his autobiography *Head or Harp* (1965): 'The republicans had blown up all the bridges over or under the track, and they crowned their efforts by destroying the big viaduct at Mallow junction on the main line between Dublin and Cork. This particular feat was ascribed to Erskine Childers (an English author with a desperately "Irish" mind) but whoever was responsible made a good job of it, for it could not be rebuilt for years. At the end of my first term in Trinity I had to travel all the way round the coast of Cork by sea; it took twenty hours and I was horribly sick'.

The Chetwynd viaduct on the Cork Bandon & South Coast line is seriously damaged by explosives, one arch being practically destroyed. All traffic ceases. On the Cork Blackrock & Passage, R. H. Good, General Manager and Engineer, reports similarly serious injury to Rochestown viaduct. All train services are stopped on this line also. The isolation of Cork is now stated to be complete. No trains have run from Dublin to Cork on the Great Southern & Western for five weeks or more, though intermittent communication between the two cities had been maintained by the D&SER via Waterford. Mails were also dispatched by this route and by sea via Liverpool, but both these channels are now closed.

Thursday 10. An armoured train [see 15 January 1923] makes its maiden trip when it participates in a roundup of Irregulars in the Birdhill area on the Ballybrophy–Limerick line. 'It consists of a wagon and an engine', according to the *Irish Independent*, 'and in the former the groundwork was a big hopper wagon, itself of tough steel and of a wedge shape calculated to minimise the effect of any explosion taking place beneath it. Over this was placed a kind of gigantic match-box, made of ¾ inch mild steel, a space being left between the inner and outer casings. In the two steel plates were cut eleven loopholes for rifles and several observation openings. In the centre of each side machine-gun ports were made, with sliding shutters. On top of the wagon was further protection, and a specially-made ladder was clamped along the roof, which could be removed to allow the garrison of this moving fort to get in and out. The engine was protected in much the same way, the cab being completely enclosed in armour plate.'

Friday 11. The 06.00 Dublin–Belfast goods is derailed at Howth Junction for the third time. Passing through Raheny it is stopped by three armed men who remove the driver, fireman and guard and, as on the previous occasions, hold open the regulator with a piece of wire sending the train full speed ahead. The guard, before descending from the van, succeeds in putting the brakes on full and when the train has travelled some distance it comes to a complete stop. The Irregulars then bring the crew back to the train and force them to release the brakes, after which they uncouple the wagons and restart the loco at maximum speed. Meanwhile seven Irregulars at Howth Junction open the points against the oncoming engine and it derails, burying itself in the ballast. A breakdown gang is quickly on the scene and Messrs Bagwell, General Manager and F. A. Campion, Chief Engineer, visit the site and inspect the damage. Passenger services continue with trains running up to each side of the blockage.

Brig. O'Daly, Free State Army, is returning to Tralee from Castleisland with troops when at Carransbridge, near Farranfore, a rail is lifted. As the train stops it comes under desultory fire from a distance, wounding Volunteer Patrick Berry, Clifden. The troops return fire and the attackers retire. R. Mellet, Stationmaster at Balla, Co. Mayo, between Claremorris and Manulla Junction, is arrested by Free State troops [see 3 October 1922].

Monday 14. Dundalk is in the possession of the Irregulars, who plan an attack on Drogheda. A train leaves Dundalk with a heavily armed contingent, estimated at 450, and heads south. Steel plates prepared under duress at the GNR Dundalk Works protect the train, which reaches Kellystown, 8 km. north of Drogheda. The Irregulars blow up an overhead bridge and tear up the line. On the Cavan & Leitrim a branch train is commandeered by the military (Free State) authorities.

Tuesday 15. Dundalk is surrounded by Free State forces. They also move out of Drogheda to face Irregulars, who have broken up into small guerrilla groups: three engagements take place. Passengers arriving from this direction at Amiens Street, Dublin, are searched by troops and six arrests are made, but there is no through communication between Dublin and Belfast until 14.00. A man who travelled from Enniskillen yesterday says that with the greatest difficulty they reached Dundalk, where they were told that the whole town, including the station, had been seized by Irregulars. He eventually reached Drogheda by car.

Two lengths of rail having been removed from just within the Wexford end of Killurin tunnel, the down Night Mail, hauled by 0-6-0 engine no. 14 *Limerick* with driver Turner and fireman O'Brien, leaves the rails but continues to run on the sleepers until she turns over. Turner is pinned inside the locomotive and is badly scalded, being unable to return to work for a year. The breakdown train arrives at 07.15 but the crew cannot prevent extensive pilfering by the local population. According to Inspector Michael Forde 'you couldn't watch 'em. They'd take anything. They came with horses and carts from far and near. Besides the coal there was a consignment of tea on the train and £300 worth of drapery goods. For long enough afterwards there was all the tea the countryside could use'. Four raiders destroy the telephone installations in the signal cabin at Enniscorthy where, in and around the tunnel, they have established an arsenal which they nickname 'Antwerp'.

With reference to the Agreement between Irish Railway Companies and the Unions, Clause 5, the Provisional Government states that, owing to the disturbed state of certain districts it has not yet been able to get into touch with a number of companies but guarantees to do so at the earliest possible moment. These include the Cork & Macroom; Cork Bandon & South Coast; Waterford & Tramore; Cork & Muskerry, including the Donoughmore Extension; Cork Blackrock & Passage; Listowel & Ballybunion; Schull & Skibbereen; Timoleague & Courtmacsherry; Ballinascarthy & Timoleague Junction and the Tralee & Dingle.

Wednesday 16. The Head Offices of the D&SER are closed from 11.00 to 14.00 to enable staff to attend the funeral of Arthur Griffith, who died suddenly in Dublin on 12 August. He led the Anglo-Irish Treaty negotiations and was elected President in place of de Valera following its ratification.

Thursday 17. The Board of the Cork & Muskerry decides 'to consider the position of the Company owing to the suspension of traffic caused by the blowing up of Leemount Bridge and Healy's Bridge. One week's notice to be given to the members of the staff paid weekly and a month's notice to the monthly paid members'. It also agrees 'to consider the running of a passenger service from each side as far as Leemount Bridge and tranship there. This would necessitate a temporary loop at Leemount for the engine to get round with the consent of the County Surveyor'. A decision is postponed. The remaining arches of Ballyvoile viaduct, blown up on the 4th last, collapse completely.

Friday 18. Free State troops return to Custume Barracks, Athlone from Lanesborough direction with nine prisoners, rifles and a large quantity of ammunition as well as some of the provisions taken from a raid on a goods train at Kiltoom, on the MGWR Westport line between Athlone and Knockcroghery, on Wednesday night. Pursuing the search for the raiders a small party of troops commandeer a Shannon steamboat.

Irregulars attack Drogheda station again. Machine gun, revolver and heavy rifle fire can be heard for over two hours in the early morning as a large body make a concerted effort to regain control of the station, attacking from three points – the north end of the viaduct, Donor's Green and the fields around Marsh Road. In the evening Mrs Esmay Young, Roden Place, Dundalk, writes to her daughter, Mrs Jeannie O'Mahony, in Drogheda. Jeannie's brother, Johnnie Young, works for the GNR in Dundalk and lives with his mother and sister in Roden Place. Mrs Young writes: 'Dear Jeannie, I got your letter and enclosure (£1) safely on Monday morning and will have Masses offered as requested but as you must be aware we had no means of communication either by wires, telephone or post since and I suppose you must think we are dead and buried but thank God we are all alive and well... I need not tell you of recent experiences and all that happened since last Monday, as you will have the true account in the [*Dundalk*] *Democrat* before perhaps you get this letter as Pat Watters says the post is going via Holyhead. The worst times we had was on Wednesday night and we spent it mostly in the cellar as the Irregulars were sniping from the Century Tower next door, from Nicholas Haughey's top window and the Distillers. We were closed up from 6o'c [she ran a tobacconist's shop] and at half nine Dr O'Hagan phoned from the Hospital that the Free State troops were on the Workhouse Hills and to send him as good supply of cigs as he would not be home...Johnny did not go to work yet and so escaped Jail, as all Railway workers and Brewery men were halted and put into clink until they were identified and it was amazing to see all the wives and mothers going up to get their husbands and sons out of prison.'

Sunday 20. John Kerr, CB&SCR General Manager, reports four bridges damaged together with the Bantry jetty and store. He has invited Messrs R. A. Skelton, who have being engaged in the company's bridge work for some years, to send over from England 'a first class bridge expert to advise on what can be done to repair or renew Chetwynd Viaduct. In consequence of the serious destruction of bridges the services of the Wages Staff will not be required after the 29th and those of the Clerical Staff would not be required after 19 September'. The workshops at Bandon and Cork are, however, to be kept open, officials of the Provisional Government having stressed the desirability of creating as little unemployment as possible.

Monday 21. Messrs News Brothers, Cork, to Eason's newsagents, Dublin: '...we are entirely cut off from connections with the rest of the country and our customers generally. All railway and road bridges have been destroyed'.

Tuesday 22. Irregulars again attempt to seize Drogheda railway station in another offensive, attacking from several points at once. A number of bombs are thrown in a conflict lasting some six hours. At Castlefinn on the County Donegal narrow gauge the signal cabin is burned to the ground. A claim of £1000 is lodged in respect of the building and contents.

The pro-Treaty *Irish Independent* editorialises: 'The railways, these days, are suffering because, like the majority of the people, they stand by the State. It is the duty of the State to see that they are not damnified. They are entitled to a subsidy to tide them over their difficulties.

Even the majority of the Commission [see 26 April 1922] cannot reasonably object to a subsidy by saying that it could not be granted without giving the State control, because their own scheme of public ownership excludes the State from control'.

Thursday 24. 'An appalling catastrophe has befallen the Irish people', according to the *Cork Examiner*: 'The nation was plunged into grief yesterday morning when the almost incredible fact became known that General Michael Collins was dead...Cork was at once plunged into mourning. All the business establishments ceased work for the day and all the trams stopped running.' The Cork & Muskerry, however, announces the provision of a limited passenger service from Coachford and Donoughmore to Leemount, the damaged bridge over the Lee, and a train from Cork to give connection at each side. The train leaves Coachford and Donoughmore at 10.00. returning from Cork at 17.00. A young boy (who will in the fullness of time assume the dignity of office as the Most Revd John J. Scanlan, DD, Auxiliary Bishop of Honolulu) uses the service to and from home and school: 'North Mon' (North Monastery), Peacock Lane: 'No train or car could get across' he is to recall in later life, 'but there was one place in the middle of the bridge over which pedestrians could pass. The "Muskerry", however, rose to the occasion by providing a train from Cork as far as the bridge to meet another train from Blarney. Everybody got out of one train to make the hazardous trip across to the other train. Footwork had to be steady, else one might find oneself in the pleasant water of the River Lee, thirty feet below. One afternoon, as we all got out to board the train on the other side, someone up on the hills around us started a machine-gun on us, or rather, I suppose, on some soldiers who were on our train. Those of us still on the road rushed into the pub (The Angler's Rest). Those who were on the train all tried to lie down on the floors of the cars. Packages were flying all over the place. Women were screaming and general pandemonium took place. The word went round that the "one-eyed gunner" was the lad responsible. He must have run out of ammunition or something because he stopped shooting. The soldiers went through the fields shooting up at the hills, and the tram pulled away towards Healy's Bridge.'

Friday 25. The Cork Blackrock & Passage assesses the cost of repairing malicious damage caused on 8 August: ticket office at Currabinny Pier, burnt down by persons unknown, £20; the ticket office and waiting room burned down at Ringaskiddy pier, £94.18.2; the roof of the stationmaster's house at Passage, damaged by Free State troops, £3; the main girders of one span of the Douglas Viaduct near Rochestown, broken by explosives, £5000.

Irregulars capture a GS&WR permanent way train with all its tools and equipment on the Mitchelstown branch. [The 20 km Fermoy–Mitchelstown branch in Co Cork was opened in March 1891 by the Fermoy & Mitchelstown Railway. Passenger traffic was terminated in January 1947 and the line saw intermittent livestock specials until its complete closure on 1 December 1953].

Saturday 26. The Ministry of Economic Affairs announces that at the special request of the Government the British & Irish Steam Packet Co. has arranged to establish a direct overnight shipping service to and from the ports of Dublin and Cork for the transportation of passengers and general cargo, including livestock. The new service will involve the running of a fast passenger vessel, of Irish registry, out of each port, initially on two or three days a week, Sunday excepted, until through rail communication is restored. The first sailing is scheduled for Wednesday next. The City of Cork Steam Packet Co. is acting as the B&I's agents in that city. The two vessels employed are the S S *Lady Kerry*, formerly simply *Kerry*, built in Port Glasgow in 1897 and S S *Bandon*, formerly *Louth*, *Lady Louth*, dating from 1894. The vessels are scheduled to sail from Sir John Rogerson's Quay, Dublin, at 17.00 (see 16 September 1922).

Monday 28. Passengers travelling from the south for the funeral of Gen. Michael Collins, shot dead in an ambush at Béal na mBláth, Co. Cork on the 22nd, are unable to get further than Kildare as the line has been broken between there and Cherryville Junction. The GS&WR had arranged day trips.

Tuesday 29. J. Coghlan, D&SER General Manager, is to convey to the Railway Transport officer at Westland Row, Dublin, the thanks of the company for the services rendered by his men at the station yesterday 'at the period of intense pressure of passengers returning from the funeral of the late General Collins'.

The GNR Board resolves that in every case of robbery by armed men, a claim be sent in to the Government concerned: there have been 11 cases of interference since 15 August. 'In view of the present state of the country and the recent theft of cash in transit', it decides, 'the Finance Committee is to investigate the possibility of an alternative method of dealing with the Company's cash receipts and payments.' Robert L. King is appointed Manager of the West Clare.

Thursday 31. At night four mines are laid on the road near Hazelhatch station, Co. Dublin and about 27 metres of the GS&WR main line – six lengths of rail – are blown up. At the same time the station is invaded and the signal cabin burned, stopping all traffic until midday. The 09.30 from Kingsbridge is run to Hazelhatch where passengers are transferred to another train south of the breach.

Friday 1. Of the Great Southern & Western hotels, Parknasilla is intact, Kenmare almost intact. The old Killarney Hotel, adjacent to the station, is occupied by Free State troops and is generally undamaged, but the new hotel in the town has been burned. [Killarney's original Great Southern Hotel, built to coincide with the opening of the railway there in 1853, was the first of its kind in Ireland (or Britain)]. Gen. Michael Brennan, O/C South Western Command, Limerick, requests the GS&WR to repair any bridges carrying the public road over the railway which have been damaged so as to provide road transport for army purposes. John F. Sides, Chief Civil Engineer, replies that the company will be ready to maintain such bridges when the County authorities restore them [see 19 April 1923].

Saturday 2. D&SER rolling stock at Harcourt Street, the Dublin terminus, suffers damage through shooting.

Sunday 3. At about 05.00 some 18 metres of track on the Dublin & Blessington are blown up and services from Terenure cannot proceed beyond Embankment. A breakdown gang arrives but is prevented from restoring the line by armed men who appear from the adjoining woods. Subsequently Free State forces reach the scene and open fire, the raiders withdrawing. Full service is restored on Monday.

Monday 4. R. H. Good, General Manager and Engineer of the Cork Blackrock & Passage, recommends the charter or purchase of an additional steamer to replace the rail service, and it is decided to charter the paddle steamer *Hibernia*, a 32 metre steel vessel built in 1904. On the West Clare, Free State troops discover a mine embedded under the sleepers between the rails about 100 metres from the Ennis side of Willbrook station. Liffey Junction signal cabin, on the MGWR in north Dublin, is set on fire by armed men and completely destroyed.

On the GS&WR a train from Cahir to Limerick Junction is held up midway between Cahir and Bansha and the passengers ordered out. Mails on board are seized. The bridge over the river Aherlow at Cappagh, between Bansha and Cahir, is burnt down and trains cannot travel beyond Bansha. The bridge, previously destroyed, has only recently been rebuilt.

16
Rathcurby – the aftermath.
See 6 May 1923.

17
Ballywilliam, Co. Wexford. The
furniture container belongs to
Messrs Anderson, Stanford &
Ridgeway, a well-known
Dublin firm.
See 6 January 1923.

18
Ballyvoile viaduct, Co. Waterford.
See 4 August 1922.

19
Members of the Railway
Protection Corps on active service
at an unidentified location.

Oglaiġ na h-Éireann

RECRUITS WANTED

FOR

RAILWAY PROTECTION, REPAIR AND

MAINTENANCE CORPS (PROTECTION BRANCH)

RECRUITS will be accepted at Corps'
Headquarters — **WELLINGTON BARRACKS;**

Or at Corps' Command Headquarters at the following places :—

GLANMIRE STATION, CORK.
LIMERICK   ,,
THURLES   ,,
CLONMEL   ,,
DUNDALK   ,,
MULLINGAR   ,,

Between the hours of 9.30 a.m. and 4 p.m., Daily.
Applicants should bring references from a Clergyman or from
present or past employer.

20
Irish Independent, 27 February 1923.

21
Ballyanne, Co. Wexford.
See 10 January 1923.

22
Ballyanne close up.

23 & 24
D&SER armoured train at Grand
Canal Street, Dublin.
See 27 March 1923.

25
'The Grey Ghost'.
See 15 October 1922.

26
Monard viaduct.
See 25 April 1923.

27
Douglas viaduct, Co. Cork.
See 25 August 1922.

28
Belvelly viaduct, Co. Cork.
See 16 March 1923.

29&30
Foynes, Co. Limerick.
See 23 April 1923.

31
Newrath, Co. Waterford.
See 25 April 1923.

32
Mountmellick, Co. Laois.
See 11 May 1923.

A motor trawler, skippered by Mr Meehan, manager of Ring Co-operative Society, carries students from Waterford to Ring Irish College, the voyage taking six hours. According to the *Waterford News* 'it seems not unlikely that this method of communication between Waterford city and West Waterford will be increasingly availed of owing to the lack of railway facilities due to blown-up bridges, etc. on the GS&WR system'.

Tuesday 5. On the MGWR the 20.30 Claremorris–Ballinrobe passenger train is held up at Carrowmore level crossing within 5 km of its destination. Armed men seize all the goods on board and the driver, fireman and guard are compelled to alight and, together with the passengers, marched under armed guard to within a short distance of Ballinrobe station where they are set at liberty. [This short branch with only one intermediate station – Hollymount – was opened by the Ballinrobe & Claremorris Light Railway in 1892 and closed completely in 1960].

Wednesday 6. The temporary signal cabin at Dalkey on the D&SER is completely burned down.

Thursday 7. The first batch of Irregular prisoners is conveyed to Gormanston internment camp, Co. Meath, by special train from Dublin. The captives number 200 and 18 of them escape on the way from the station to the camp. Only eight are subsequently recaptured. [Gormanstown, a former British military base, had been made available by their remaining forces to supplement the military prison at Kilmainham, Dublin. As the number of prisoners increased in the course of the conflict, enquiries were made of the British as to the possibility of transhipping internees to St Helena or the Seychelles].

Friday 8. The temporary signal cabin and waiting accomodation at Macmine Junction are burnt. [Macmine Junction was exclusively a railway facility with no public access by road. The junction for Waterford off the D&SER Dublin-Wexford line, it opened in 1873 and closed, with the Waterford line, in 1964]. At 02.00 armed men arrive at Emly station on the main Dublin–Cork line and order the stationmaster and three signalmen to vacate their premises. The stationmaster persuades the raiders to spare the dwelling-house, but the other buildings are completely burnt out. He succeeds in rescuing the goods, tickets and money from his office. The goods store contained about 16 tons of flour and other foodstuffs.

Saturday 9. The first meeting of the new Dáil, elected on 16 June. A force of 84 Irregulars capture the town of Kenmare, Co. Kerry, with the objective of securing provisions and arms. One of their number, Jeremiah Murphy, recalls: 'we proceeded towards the objective mostly along the railway tracks, with our equipment piled on hand-cars. It was a pitch dark night and all went well until two hand-cars collided while coasting at about thirty miles an hour. Suddenly the lead car was derailed at a spot where some railway track had been torn up. About fifteen men were pitched to the bottom of a steep bank, amid all sorts of gear, but none of them was hurt…The [Kenmare] railway station was our command post'.

Monday 11. P. J. Holden, the D&SER agent at Palace East, Co Wexford, is arrested by Free State troops. [see 10 October 1922].

Tuesday 12. Eighteen D&SER employees are recorded as having been 'absent from duty for some considerable time through political causes'. M. F. Keogh, General Manager, reports that Curfew Regulations have been withdrawn in Waterford but that in consideration of the very few passengers using the last up and down trains between Waterford and Macmine before the Curfew came into force, and that since the withdrawal of the Curfew no applications have been made for its restoration he has not restored the service. Delay to some of the Kingstown [Dun Laoghaire] Pier trains has occurred in consequence of the enginemen being unable to come on duty at the proper time owing to heavy firing in the vicinity of the Grand Canal Street depot, Dublin, at night.

Wednesday 13. Lady Gregory travels to Dublin: 'Trains slow, journey took 12.30 to 7.30 including two hours wait at Athenry.' The D&SER's agent at Glenmore station is arrested but later released. The Minister of Industry & Commerce writes to the C-in-C, Gen. Richard Mulcahy: 'We have been informed by our Transport Department that the armed men, who burned the station and goods store at Emly on the G&SWR on the 8th instant, stated that they were being instructed to burn all railway stations. We consider it desirable to inform you of this matter in case you may wish to take suitable action.'

Thursday 14. The Cork Blackrock & Passage line remains closed: there has been no traffic for the past week. Rolls Royce, Peerless and Lancia armoured cars, which have been operating on a 'freelance' basis, are formally organised under Capt. Joe Hyland as O/C Armoured Car Corps to constitute the Cavalry Corps.

Saturday 16. A stormy night on the east coast. Enniscorthy signal cabin is attacked and burnt. The instruments controlling the goods yard are put out of commission but are repaired on Sunday evening to enable fair day traffic to be handled on Monday 21. The breakdown crew arrives from Wexford at 19.00 and has completed the work by 23.00.

'Dubliniensis' writes to the editor, *Irish Independent*: 'Sir, the announcement of daily services henceforth between Dublin and Cork by the B & I Steampacket Co. is a very welcome one.

The fare (£3 return) is altogether excessive compared with the rail fare...I have just had to send my entire family away to Cork by this route and the fare totalled £16 10s' [see 26 August 1922].

Monday 18. The annual Harvest Fair takes place in Collooney, Co. Sligo. In the evening a special cattle train leaves the town. As it descends a steep gradient halfway between Collooney and Dromahair on the Sligo Leitrim & Northern Counties line the driver sees a signal at red and beyond it crossing gates closed across the line. He ignores the signal and as the train crashes through the gates a dozen Irregulars signal him to stop – a few shots are fired. They explain that they intend to derail the train in order to prevent Free State troops using the line. The driver asks to be allowed to proceed to Dromahair, and this is conceded, a number of Irregulars joining the train. At Dromahair the driver asks them what is to be the fate of the cattle when the train is derailed. The problem is simply solved: empty wagons are coupled to the rear of the train which then proceeds to a point a few hundred metres beyond Dromahair. The empties are uncoupled, the Irregulars tear up the line behind the train and the driver shunts the wagons into the gap. The special continues uneventfully with its bovine cargo to Enniskillen.

At Athlone, Lady Gregory's down train from Dublin is shunted and stopped outside the station. 'A woman looking out of the window said there were coffins. I looked out and saw them, three I think. Men were lifting them on their shoulders'.

Wednesday 20. In the evening the first train for 13 weeks runs between Thurles and Limerick Junction on the GS&WR. A group of armed men again hold up a train near Bansha (see 4 September) and take out all on board. They say that another group has gone to hold up a goods train coming from the opposite direction and that the two trains would be set in motion so as to collide with each other. After some time, however, there is no sign of the goods, so the passenger coaches are sprinkled with petrol and set on fire. The evicted travellers are obliged to walk either to Tipperary or Cahir, leaving their luggage in country houses. The engine is partially wrecked but the driver succeeds in bringing it back under its own power to Tipperary station.

Thursday 21. The Cork & Muskerry reports receipts for the week ending September 8 at £131; wages £261. Figures for the following week are receipts £115, wages £265.

Friday 22. Large boulders are placed on the Burtonport line of the Letterkenny & Burtonport Extension beyond Dunfanaghy Road and the telegraph lines cut. A number of men hand a driver employed at the place a notice threatening 'severe penalties' if the obstructions are removed from the per. way. Trains are delayed about an hour while the line is cleared.

Saturday 23. Crumlin bridge on the GS&WR Athenry–Claremorris line near Ballyglunin station is completely destroyed and three others blown up. The track is extensively damaged.

Monday 25. Dundrum station, D&SER, is raided by armed men. On the MGWR a down special of livestock ex Boyle is held up by armed men between Kilfree and Ballymote. The engine is uncoupled from the train and the driver ordered to re-start it whereupon it runs for about 3 km. The 12.30 goods is following and is brought to a stand at the same point where the wagons are raided, two casks of porter being removed.

Memo to Gen. Mulcahy, C-in-C, from Colonel C. F. Russell, seeking authority to organise 'a Corps for the purpose of Protecting, Repairing and Maintaining in Repair the Railways'. [Charles Russell, who had served in the 1914–18 war as an RAF pilot, worked subsequently on railways in Canada before returning to Ireland and becoming responsible for the acquisition, during the Anglo-Irish Treaty negotiations in London in 1921, of an aircraft which would be kept on standby to enable Michael Collins and his colleagues to make a hasty departure should the negotiations fail. The aircraft, a Martynside Mark II 'A', nicknamed, after Collins, 'The Big Fella', was not ultimately required for this purpose and was crated and shipped to Dublin, arriving at Baldonnel aerodrome in June 1922. It became the first machine owned and operated by the nascent Air Corps. Russell was made responsible for organising civil aviation under the Provisional Government but was seconded from this role to command the Railway Preservation, Maintenance and Repair Corps of the Free State army. In July 1922 he had instigated air patrols of the railways from Baldonnel in response to Irregular attacks].

A Lancia car carrying Free State troops from Portobello barracks collides with a Donnybrook tram at Baggott Street bridge, Dublin. Nine people are slightly injured, the car is overturned and the tram derailed.

Tuesday 26. Colonel Russell is authorised by the C-in-C 'to have the Corps armed, uniformed and properly instructed in musketry; to recruit therefore unemployed railway men of all grades, preferably those unemployed who are not receiving benefit on any kind and, if necessary, and to a restricted extent, railway officials at present employed; to recruit also for the Corps men other than railway men; to make temporary appointments in the Corps up to the rank of Commandant, strict attention being paid to the fact that only men acting in command of a number of Companies shall have the rank of Commandant; to arrange with the various GOCs for the immediate protection of important bridges and tunnels, from the troops at present at their disposal, until such time as these troops can be relieved by men from the Railway Corps, and to have altered up to 12 Lancia cars for patrol work on the railways'.

Wednesday 27. Seapoint station on the D&SER suburban line is raided by armed men and 19 shillings taken.

Thursday 28. The General Manager of the CB&SCR informs his board that a proposal has been made by the military authorities 'to raise a battalion of railwaymen to be armed and used for the repair, maintenance and protection of the line. The men are to be paid by the companies and the material required is to be issued in the ordinary way, the Government to repay the companies for both at short intervals, a procedure which would cancel the claims for malicious injuries'. The suggestion, he says, has not been too well received by the men and is full of practical difficulties, and after a few interviews General Dalton has postponed taking action in the matter for a few days. Emmet Dalton, (1898–1978) nicknamed 'Ginchy' on account of his bravery when serving with the British in the 1914–18 war, was in charge of the bombardment of the Four Courts and is now, as from August, GOC Southern Command. He sends a message to the C-in-C, Portobello: 'Send Russell immediately to deal with railway matters.' C-in-C replies (from Cork): 'Will arrange about Russell who is at present finishing up details of scheme with the Railway Authorities here.'

Announcing alterations to many services as from Monday next, 2 October, M. F. Keogh, General Manager, Midland Great Western, advises prospective passengers that 'the Night Mail Trains to and from Dublin have been temporarily discontinued. The train service on the Galway–Clifden and Westport–Achill branches have had to be suspended owing to prevailing circumstances'. The GS&WR announces the extension of its main line service to Mallow 'which must be the terminus for a considerable time owing to the destruction of the viaduct there, the repair of which must occupy at least six months. The line from Mallow to Kerry is still closed, and the Rosslare line is also broken in Co. Wexford. Yesterday morning the line was again broken between Gowran and Bagenalstown, but a passenger service is being maintained to and from this point of obstruction...'

Friday 29. Russell is losing no time. He signals the C-in-C: 'I have pleasure in informing you that the first Lancia car converted for railway work is a complete success. This afternoon, during trials, we obtained a forward speed of 45 miles an hour and a rear speed of 20 miles an hour. As previously arranged we are proceeding with the conversion of 11 other cars.' The Lancias, fitted with flanged wheels and armament, are to play a vital role in the activities of the Railway Corps.

The 16.30 D&SER train from Dublin is ambushed between Killurin and Wexford and damage done to two carriages.

'APOLOGY TO THE SHOPPING PUBLIC': Phelan Bros., George's Street, Waterford, announce that their 'GREAT ANNUAL SALE OF COLOSSAL STOCKS begins Friday October 6th. No doubt a huge volume of the Shopping public of Waterford and District have been somewhat disappointed that our usual popular Annual Sale has not been announced long before now, but owing to the disturbed conditions prevailing during the Summer months, and the consequent dislocation of Railway facilities etc., we did not hold our Summer sale...'

Saturday 30. Russell dispatches a memo to Government informing them of the formation of the RPR&MC and seeking as 'urgently necessary' the securing by the Trade and Commerce Ministry of an engineer 'for the purpose of advising in all matters concerning the reconstruction of various portions of the line, and whose opinions, as against that of the Railway Companies' Engineers, the Government would be prepared to stand by'. He also requests the outlining on behalf of the Ministry of the financial policy in the matter. The first command to be established has been organised at Thurles and it is proposed to repair Thurles–Clonmel line in the early days of next month.

D&SER no. 56 *Rathmines* built 1895, withdrawn 1934.

PER. WAY MEN AND PORTERS?

Sunday 1. The down evening train from Dublin on the D&SER is ambushed as it leaves Killurin station, Co. Wexford. Twelve soldiers on board reply to rifle fire with a Lewis gun but no damage is sustained and there are no casualties. The Midland Great Western Inagh Lodge hotel is broken into and all the furniture carted away. The Dublin United Tramways' depots at Clonskea, Donnybrook, Dartry and Terenure are raided by armed men, who take a sum of £3 9s.9d. from Clonskea.

The Cork Blackrock & Passage introduces a revised timetable for its Greenboat steamer services on the Cork–Passage–Monkstown–Cobh (Queenstown)–Aghada–Crosshaven route. The Hon. the Recorder of Cork KC awards the company £6,975 at Cork East Riding Quarter Sessions in respect of the destruction of Douglas bridge (£7177 9s was claimed). He cannot, he says, compensate for the damage done by Free State troops at Passage.

Monday 2. In a memorandum to the Railway Protection Corps Gen. Mulcahy, C-in-C, advises that 'Dr Crowley, in his capacity as Government Consulting Engineer, will take responsibility for controlling executively whatever part of this work that requires to be so controlled, and advising in respect of other portions of the work'.

Tuesday 3. A large tree put across the line at Myshall on the Cork & Muskerry delays the Coachford train for one hour. Ganger Connell is required to submit a written explanation to the board as to why the tree was not removed before the passage of the train. The bridge across the Shannon at Drumsna on the MGWR is blown up. Near Ballyhale station on the Kilkenny–Waterford line a bomb is thrown at an evening train. As it leaves the station the driver sees some individuals at the lineside acting in a suspicious manner. When the train passes them one man hurls a missile which lands inside a full carriage. Seated with the civilian passengers are Lieuts. Foley and O'Rourke of the Free State army who promptly dispose of the bomb through a window before it can explode.

In the Dáil, Liam Ó Daimhín (Laois-Offaly) asks the Minister for Defence, Richard Mulcahy, 'whether he is aware that on the entry of Free State troops into Balla, Co. Mayo on 11 August, the Officer in Charge placed the stationmaster, Mr R. Mellet, under arrest, without giving him time to close the office or lock up the cash on hands, amounting to over £400; whether

Mr Mellet was detained in a stable for five days and nights, without removing his clothes or without sleeping accommodation of any kind; whether, on the following Sunday, he was paraded through the streets to attend mass, covered with a revolver, with his clothes smeared with the dirt of the stable and without being permitted to wash or shave for five days; whether, at the end of that period he was released, with a statement that he had been arrested on local information, which was found to be incorrect...' In the absence of the Minister for Defence the question is not answered. [Richard Mulcahy, it should be noted, occupies the dual roles of Minister and Commander-in-Chief].

Wednesday 4. The Coachford train is again held up at Dripsey, and rails are removed at Magurla. At Woodenbridge on the D&SER the signal cabin is set on fire and the wires cut, but the damage is slight. On the same line a bomb is thrown into the Avoca signal box: all the glass is broken and the phone damaged. Further south, Inch station is raided and considerable damage done to the premises.

Thursday 5. President Cosgrave announces that as the local authorities will in many cases be unable to meet the claims for malicious injuries, the Government proposes to assume, as far as the railways are concerned, a limited liability for reconstruction subject to their control of design and expenditure. The General Manager of the CB&SCR is appointed to a committee of engineers to confer with the Government engineers on the question of repairs and renewals of bridges. Representatives of the Cork & Muskerry meet officials of the Ministry of Economic Affairs with regard to wages paid to staff during the emergency train service. It is agreed that where possible the entire staff work every alternate week only; and any of the staff that can be dispensed with are to be put off temporarily. The Blarney stationmaster is to be kept on as caretaker at half his present salary. The Clonmel–Waterford line is now in a fit state to be reopened to traffic.

In the Dáil, Tomás Ó Conaill (Galway) asks the Minister for Industry & Commerce, Joseph McGrath, whether he is aware of the very great hardship which exists in Tuam and the surrounding neighbourhood owing to the difficulty of getting food and other commodities into the town, consequent on the closing down of the railway and the destruction of road bridges; whether the railway line from Athenry to Tuam and Sligo has been closed down for three months and over 300 men thrown out of employment. Kevin O'Higgins, replying for the Minister, admits that it is a fact that there have been serious interruptions of railway and road communications in the Tuam district: 'I am in communication with the Great Southern & Western Co. in order to expedite repairs, and also with the military authorities, since the extent to which it is practicable to carry out repairs largely depends on what protection can be afforded.'

Friday 6. The General Manager of the D&SER reports that the first boiler of the two 6-wheel coupled goods engines, contracted for by Board Order 25144, has been tested in steam by the Locomotive Engineer. In consequence of the burning of signal cabins at the southern end of the line the Winter train service came into operation on 25 September, not 1 October as originally intended. Clerk D. O'Callaghan, Enniscorthy, having been elected a TD, has been absent without leave since 8 September. He is granted leave of absence for two months and is to be found work temporarily at Harcourt Street or Westland Row, Dublin.

The GS&WR drivers based in Cork request that the company should allow them to borrow from the amount standing to their credit in the Enginemen's Fund to tide them over the present difficulties. This is agreed. Messrs Sir William Arrol & Co.'s tender for the erection of a temporary bridge over the Blackwater at Mallow in the sum of £18,125 is also agreed. The Traffic & Works Committee suggests that it is the responsibility of the Government to find the expense of renewals of damage and regrets that adequate protection has not been provided in the past. E. A. Neale, General Manager, seeks guidance on the question of re-employing men who have been arrested by the Free State forces and released on signing an undertaking to cease further hostile activities. He is told that such cases may be considered as and when vacancies arise. John Sides, Chief Civil Engineer, asks for a direction as to whether the erection of signal cabins should be proceeded with, having regard to their continued destruction. He is told that preparations should be made but actual erection postponed. A gang of men repairing bridge 103 between Bagenalstown [Muine Bheag] and Gowran come under attack.

Sunday 8. At Salthill station on the Dublin & South Eastern four men enter the signal cabin and order the signalman out. They then pour petrol on the woodwork and set it alight, warning the signalman not to move for 20 minutes and telling him that there is a bomb in the cabin. When they leave he finds that the woodwork is only scorched and there is no bomb.

Monday 9. A motor car containing four men and one woman dashes through the level crossing gates south of Stillorgan, Co. Dublin as the 16.30 train from Bray is approaching them. The driver turns the car onto a plot of ground beside the line and the occupants thereupon leave it and board the train for Dublin, refusing either to give their names or pay their fares. The incident is reported to the military.

Tuesday 10. The Catholic hierarchy's joint pastoral condemns Republican [Irregular] resistance to the Free State. A flying column of 16 Irregulars enters Drogheda on bicycles from a northern direction. They link up with other anti-Treaty troops and the telegraph wires to Dundalk and Dublin are cut. They then launch simultaneous attacks against Free State troops on the Boyne viaduct, the railway station and Millmount. The patrol at the northern end of the viaduct comes under heavy fire from the quays and retreat back across the bridge only to have bombs hurled at them from the fields on the southern side. The railway station comes under fire from a Thompson machine gun well as Mausers, revolvers and bombs.

The MGWR hotel at Recess is burnt out. The hotel, on the Galway–Clifden line, has its own platform, opened in 1902 but closed when the building is burnt. On the West Clare, Cullenagh road bridge is damaged: 'the most dangerous outrage yet committed on the line' in the view of the management. The Cork Command of the Railway Protection, Repair & Maintenance Corps is established at Glanmire station, GS&WR.

On the GS&WR main line prospective passengers are availing of a motor service between Cork and Buttevant and goods are being transported by motor lorries. Between Thurles and Fethard, Irregular attacks on a breakdown train, guarded by an armoured train and other troops, engaged in repairing bridges and track, have abated. The officer and seven men missing since an attack on the train last week have reported at Fethard.

In the Dáil, Domhnall Ó Ceallacháin (Wexford) asks the Minister for Defence if he is aware that the stationmaster at Palace East, Co. Wexford, was arrested by Free State troops on 11 September and has since been detained in New Ross barracks without charge or trial, and if he is prepared to put this man on trial or alternatively release him, since he is the sole support of his mother and sister. Gen. Mulcahy replies that Mr P. J. Holden was arrested on suspicion that he was co-operating persistently with Irregulars, who were active in that area. On the 7 October he was formally advised that he was released, having signed 'the usual form of undertaking'.

Thursday 12. The military authorities have requisitioned one of the CB&SCR Company's engines and require it to be armoured. The Locomotive Engineer is proceeding with this work.

Friday 13. The GS&WR receives a request from Galway County Council to the effect that the company repair certain bridges carrying public roads over the railway. The company replies that it will undertake such work on receipt of the necessary funding from the County Council, adding that in all cases an application is to be made to the Council for payment in respect of malicious raids. The Arrol contract for the proposed bridge over the Blackwater has been cancelled by Dr Crowley on the instructions of the Government and this will be confirmed in writing by the Minister for Industry and Commerce. The Arrol contract was for a rebuilding in stone, but the replacement, to be built by Armstrong Whitworth of Newcastle-on-Tyne, will be of standard steel construction.

Men are engaged in repairing bridges near Carrick-on-Suir and it is expected that rail communication will be re-established with Clonmel within a week and with Waterford during the next fortnight. It is nearly four months since a train entered or left Carrick and since the line was put out of action in July the quays and roads, according to the *Waterford News*, 'have daily witnessed sights that were familiar to the eyes of the grandfathers of the present inhabitants of the town, viz. long lines of carts laden with every class of goods going from the boats to all the towns and villages in South Tipperary'.

Sunday 15. Under Emergency Powers legislation military courts are now empowered to impose the death penalty. A Lancia car fitted with flanged wheels by the Railway Protection Corps and nicknamed *Grey Ghost*, O/C Lieut. Quinlan, is ambushed at first light by about a dozen Irregulars under Bill Quirke whilst patrolling the line between Thurles and Clonmel. [Opened in 1880 under the ambitious title of the Southern of Ireland Railway, it was in fact worked by the Waterford Limerick & Western until that concern was taken over by the GS&WR in 1901. At this time effectively the principal route between Clonmel and Dublin, the line subsequently lost most of its traffic and was to close completely in 1967, evidence of its physical existence now almost entirely obliterated]. Having failed on its passage to Thurles to explode a mine planted by the attackers, on its way back the Lancia is blocked by a stone barrier and its retreat cut off behind by coping stones dislodged from a bridge west of Moyglass. Fire opened on the car is returned until the crew run out of ammunition for its Lewis gun and surrender, being relieved of their weapons, ammunition and greatcoats. The Lancia is set on fire and partially burned. According to one account, both attackers and defenders thereupon adjourn to a convenient public house in Moyglass and drink each other's health; but according to driver Martin White, the Irregulars 'marched the prisoners to the home of my cousin, and gave her £2 for their refreshments and medical needs, as some of them were slightly wounded. They were then allowed to go...' [See 9 November 1922].

Monday 16. A strike of general traffic staff begins at 05.00 and closes the GS&WR Works at Inchicore and Kingsbridge and North Wall stations. Under the February agreement between management and unions the men were given a guaranteed week whether there was work on offer or not. Owing to the great reduction in business resulting from serious damage to the system the guaranteed week has been suspended for some weeks, the men being paid four or five days per week according to the manpower required by the traffic offering. However, drivers and firemen at Inchicore have been given six days' guarantee for this present week and the traffic men are claiming the same. Management maintain that the question of how many staff are needed at any given time is a matter for them, and at a meeting between the two sides before the Minister for Labour last Saturday no agreement was forthcoming. Both termini close completely to traffic but some incoming trains reach Kingsbridge and others are unloaded at Inchicore. Some 590 men are involved, including porters, shunters, cleaners, guards, ticket checkers and men employed in the goods and coaching depots. Signalmen at Inchicore are also out. Drivers and firemen report for duty but are unable to take out trains. At Kingsbridge the usual guard of Free State troops at strategic points remains on duty and later in the day pickets are posted.

The telephone apparatus at Fintown station on the County Donegal is smashed. [The station, opened in 1895 and closed in 1947, is now the base for a heritage railway. The Stranorlar–Glenties line closed to all traffic in 1952].

Tuesday 17. F. Kennedy of the MGWR has joined the Free State Army but intends to resume his pupilage on the termination of the present crisis. He asks that an allowance be made him for the period absent. A similar concession was granted to pupils in the Locomotive Department during the recent European War.

Thursday 19. F. W. Vereker, Assistant Locomotive Engineer of the Cork Bandon & South Coast, reports that 15 men were kept working on Monday last and six on Tuesday to finish the armour-plating of no. 3 engine, handed over to the military authorities the same day. On the MGWR the 07.15 goods, Athlone–Ballina, is held up 5 km outside Athlone and a considerable quantity of items removed from the wagons. A dispatch from Capt. J. Farrell, HQ No. 3 Brigade, Adamson Castle, Athlone to Railway Protection Corps' headquarters reads: 'Acting on instructions received I proceeded with Capts. Rattigan and Carroll and a party of 26 men to Coosan [on the Westmeath shore of Lough Ree] to search for looted goods. I raided several likely houses and searched woods around thoroughly and also touched islands but found no trace of anything. On the following day with the same party I carried out a search on the Connaught side of the river at Purts [Ports] village and learned that the goods raided from the train had been taken away immediately afterwards. I then searched woods and bog stretching from Purts to Kiltoom but found nothing. I learned that the following are very active in this district: Doyle, Burns, Pender, Ready. Returned to Athlone via Curnaseer village where we made further searches.'

The GS&WR strike continues. The Strike Committee of the Irish Transport & General Workers' Union, referring to a statement by E. A. Neale, General Manager, regarding the refusal of the pickets to allow perishable goods to be removed, state that they have endeavoured, where possible, to facilitate traders in getting away perishable goods received prior to the strike, but that consignments arriving after its commencement will not be handled.

Friday 20. GS&WR milesmen at Kingsbridge and North Wall and in the two gangs on the North Wall branch have also ceased work. At North Wall men are paid off after receiving the 'week in hand' wages held by the company until the termination of engagements – the normal practice. Coal cargoes cannot be discharged from vessels for want of wagons and long trains of loaded wagons occupy the sidings, unable to depart.

In the Dáil, Domhnaill Ó Ceallacháin (Wexford) asks the Minister for Industry & Commerce if he is aware 'that large sections of many of the railways in the south and south-west of the country are completely closed down, as the companies allege that they are unable to maintain a service owing to the conditions obtaining in these districts, the result being that some thousands of railway employees are unemployed and many of them are on the verge of starvation'. Replying, Joseph McGrath concedes that considerable numbers of railwaymen have lost their employment but, 'at the suggestion of the men, arrangements have been made to employ a substantial proportion of them on the work of repairing and maintaining the lines'.

Sunday 22. Percy A. Hay, Secretary, MGWR, receives a letter from the distraught manageress of the Mallaranny hotel on the Westport–Achill line: 'Dear Sir, I am sorry to have to tell you that the IRA are taking away the fresh-water Boiler. They are in the house since last Monday. As far as I can say they have taken it over but have not sent us away. They are working at the taking out of the Boiler all the week and will be for several days yet – about 100. I do not know what to put on the Return without writing you all they had and done. The Larder wall is broken down – anyone can go in there now. All gates are open day and night and the cows and donkeys of the village are destroying the grounds. The electric light is on day and night all over the place. We are having an awful time. Yrs. faithfully, A. F. Brosnan.'

On the Cork & Muskerry, receipts for the week ending 14 October total £112, wages £189. All men at present employed on full time are to be informed that a reduction of 25 per cent must be enforced if the railway is to continue to run.

Monday 23. On the MGWR Ballinrobe branch the large iron bridge spanning the Robe river between Claremorris and Hollymount is blown up for the fourth time by two mines. The explosion is heard 13 km off. The morning train from Ballinrobe reaches the bridge and the passengers are obliged to walk the rest of the way to Claremorris. The train returns and all traffic is suspended.

Tuesday 24. The GNR is to make representation to the Minister of Commerce, Government of Northern Ireland, as to delays, and consequent injury to the trade of the country, occasioned by constant searching of trains. Authority is given for the issue of an 'All Stations' Annual Pass to

Capt. Sir Basil Brooke, Bart., Deputy Chairman, Clogher Valley Railway [the future Lord Brookborough and Prime Minister of Northern Ireland]. There have been five cases of interference since 11 October.

Thomas Elliott, Traffic Manager, MGWR, writes to Richard Mulcahy in his capacity as Minister of Defence: 'I have to inform you that on the night of the 20th inst. a number of armed men visited Ballinasloe station and compelled the Station Master to surrender money to the amount of £36.19s.2d. The Station Master further reports that these men threatened him and gave him seven days' notice in which to clear out of Ballinasloe. I shall be glad if you will take the necessary action in regard to this matter and arrange to have some protection afforded for this station by night.' Another letter is addressed by Percy A. Hay, Secretary, to Kevin O'Higgins, Minister of Home Affairs, enclosing a copy of the Mallaranny Manageress's letter of 22 October: 'My directors would be glad if the Government could take some steps to protect the Company's property. Only the other day their hotel at Recess, Connemara, was burned down and they fear that if some steps are not taken Mallaranny may share the same fate.'

The Government, in the person of Joseph McGrath, Minister for Industry & Commerce, is also in receipt of correspondence from E. A. Neale, General Manager, GS&WR, to the effect that 'The Company wish me to convey to the Government their appreciation of the services rendered by the Railway Protection, Repair and Maintenance Service in opening and keeping open for traffic the lines from Thurles to Clonmel. They recognise that at the moment repair work on the Branch partakes of the nature of a Military operation, but so far as they can ascertain repairs can be carried out on the other sections mentioned [in a letter dated 20.10 from Russell to J. F. Sides, Chief Engineer] by the Company's men. On the other hand they wish to point out that they are informed that the repair of the lines between Nenagh and Birdhill and between Mallow and Tralee can only be undertaken as Military operations, and the early opening of the former section is specially important from the Company's point of view. PS. I have since heard that the Nenagh and Birdhill line has been repaired, the local Military Authorities having afforded us the necessary protection'.

The Railway Arbitration Commission announces the allocation of the grant of £3,900,000 made by the British treasury to the Irish railways following the ending of Control (15 August 1921). Arbitration was made necessary by the companies failing to agree as to the distribution of the money.

Wednesday 25. The report of the Commission of Enquiry into Irish Railways, already widely leaked, is officially issued (see 26 April 1922). The attempts to end the GS&WR strike have so far failed but are being continued. A quantity of butter, bacon and other foodstuffs is removed from Kingsbridge under permit from the ITGWU strike committee. Picketing continues at Kingsbridge and North Wall termini.

A train travelling between Kilsheelan and Clonmel on the GS&WR Limerick–Waterford line is halted by a red light and the passengers and crew ordered off. The loco is detached and run ahead for some distance, stopped, reversed and run back into the carriages, telescoping them. An unsuccessful attempt is also made to derail a passenger train from Thurles to Clonmel by placing rocks on the line. Part of the locomotive of the breakdown train derailed between Milltown and Ballindine on the Tuam–Clarremorris line and run into a bog has been blown up and the van wrecked. [Tuam–Claremorris was opened in 1894/5 by the Athenry & Tuam Extension to Claremorris Light Railway. Passenger services were withdrawn on 5 April 1976 but the track remains in situ and the line is scheduled for re-opening].

Thursday 26. Further to Percy Hay's letter, the Secretary of the Ministry of Home Affairs writes to the Minister of Defence: 'in view of the fact that the [MGWR] Company's other hotel at Recess has recently been burned down and as it has been found impossible to send the Civic Guard as yet to that district, the Minister will be glad if you will be so good as to have the necessary instructions issued so that everything possible may be done to afford protection to the Hotel in question.' The GS&WR's line from Sligo to Claremorris is ready for traffic but the light engine dispatched from Sligo for the purpose of working the morning train from Claremorris is held up at Curry station by armed men and has to return to Sligo. The opening of the branch has in consequence to be abandoned for the present.

The Tralee & Fenit railway sees its first train for two months. Two specials run to Fenit pier, returning with badly-needed fuel and foodstuffs for the town. The congestion on the pier is cleared and ships are again able to discharge into railway wagons.

Friday 27. C-in-C to Gen. Seán McMahon, Chief of Staff: 'Will you please arrange to have Russell instructed to be in Dublin on Wednesday 1st November with a view to seeing to where we are generally with regard to his work... the question of protecting a very large number of bridges in the whole of the South and sustaining this protection for some length of time has now arisen... we shall have to make general plans for this work right away.' Repairs to the bridge between Tralee and Ardfert on the line to Listowel and Limerick, damaged on 31 August and 1 September, are put in hands but when the work is close to completion fire is opened on the gangers from the hills in the neighbourhood. They take shelter for a while but on resuming work are again fired on and the repairs have to be abandoned. The next morning it is found that the bridge has again been broken down.

Saturday 28. From the Minister of Finance [W. T. Cosgrave] to the Minister of Defence [Richard Mulcahy]: 'The Minister is gravely perturbed by the very rapid increase in the expenditure of the Army generally and he trusts that if the Corps is formed at all, expenditure upon it will be kept within narrow limits. There would appear to be considerable danger, unless the limits of the Corps' operations are rigidly defined, that the Railway Companies will use it as a means of evading their own obligations to carry out repairs, and also as an opportunity of reducing their wage bill...It is clearly desirable that the more highly paid grades of Railwaymen should be excluded from the Corps as far as possible, and after consultation with the Transport Department, the Minister suggests that enrolment in the Corps should be restricted as far as possible to permanent-way men and porters.' [After the war, Col. Russell was to observe that the Army quartermastering was 'simply diabolical...when I was in charge of the Railway Corps I had two enemies – one was the Irregulars and the other was the QMG'].

The GS&WR District Engineer proceeds with the repair train to the section between Tuam and Claremorris but it is seized by Irregular forces and badly derailed. There are now two engines lying derelict on this portion of the line.

Monday 30. The Inchicore Works of the GS&WR closes, throwing 1500 workers idle. No trains have run in or out of Kingsbridge or North Wall for a fortnight with the result that no work for them is available. Mallow station is set on fire and is now in ruins, including the parcel and booking offices, refreshment rooms, waiting rooms and the stationmaster's residence. Services to Cork from Dublin, Limerick and Waterford are suspended. The bridge near Kilmorna on the GS&WR North Kerry line between Abbeyfeale and Listowel is burnt and traffic interrupted.

Tuesday 31. Between Cahir and Clonmel on the GS&WR the 15.00 passenger train is brought to a halt by a red flag and detonators. A number of men appear and tell passengers and crew to leave the train, removing mails and parcels from the guard's van. They then lift a section of track, detach the engine, run it forward and reverse it at high speed into the train, telescoping some carriages and wrecking others. This operation is repeated three times until the coaches are completely demolished. The stranded passengers make their way as best they can to the nearest towns.

THE JOB'S OXO

Wednesday 1. At Killurin, the up Wexford mail is again ambushed at the ballast pit a kilometre or so north of the station. Tom (Sandy) Hogan, with Jack Rogan firing, is driving no. 67 *Rathmore*, a 4-4-0 dating from 1905. As they round the curve at about 80 kph they see a barrier built of eight or ten sleepers with red flags flying from the corners. The locomotive strikes the blockage, totally demolishing it and is brought to a stop some distance further on. Two Army officers on board the train jump to the ground and double back down the line, firing as they go. The raiders flee. The locomotive, though damaged, succeeds in reaching Macmine Junction, where no. 67 is replaced and the train continues to Dublin. Michael Forde, D&SER Permanent Way Inspector for the Wexford area, travels back to the town in the company of Commdt. Gallagher, O/C Wexford, who, expecting another attack as their train passes through Killurin, places two Mill's bombs at the ready. They are not required.

Sallins Junction on the GS&WR is raided, the telephone broken in the signal cabin and the wires cut. A Railway Corps advance party arrives at Limerick and takes up guard duties at the station.

In the Dáil, Tomás Ó Conaill (Galway) asks the Minister for Industry & Commerce, Joseph McGrath, if he is aware that considerable inconvenience is caused to the business people and residents of Galway and the West of Ireland generally by the discontinuance of the night mail trains on the Midland Great Western. The Minister replies that he has been in touch with the company which has informed him that in view of the present disturbed conditions it has cancelled all night trains on its system and that all traffic is now worked during daylight hours.

Thursday 2. Dublin. A conference on damage to bridges is held at the Government Offices. Present on behalf of the Government are President Cosgrave; General Mulcahy, National Defence; Colonel Charles Russell; Joseph McGrath, Labour, Industry & Commerce, Economic Affairs; Mr Brennan, Gordon Campbell, John Ingram and Dr Crowley, Consulting Engineer. Representing the railway companies are Sir William Goulding, Bart., Chairman, GS&WR and his General Manager, E. A. Neale; Major Cusack, Chairman, MGWR and General Manager M. F. Keogh; John Fane Vernon, Chairman and John Bagwell, General Manager, GNR; Sir Thomas Grattan Esmonde, Chairman, D&SER and Mr Maguire; J. R. Kerr; General Manager, CB&SCR; R. H. Good, General Manager & Engineer, Cork Blackrock & Passage. It is proposed 'that the Railway Companies will themselves carry out all repairs not involving the letting of a contract or the engagement of additional labour unless notified by the Railway Maintenance Corps that a particular repair, being in the nature of a military operation, will be carried out by the Corps'. The question of whether the Corps will deal with permanent repairs only provokes disagreement and is postponed for further consideration.

On the CB&SCR there is more damage caused to Mutton Bank Bridge near Drimoleague by explosives. It is decided to contribute a sum of £50 to a fund being raised by the staff for certain members of the clerical staff whose service has had to be dispensed with owing to the closing of the line, and who are in straitened circumstances in consequence. The line is still closed.

The 06.45 GNR Limited Mail ex Dublin is stopped by eight armed men at Malahide. They have previously removed the signalman from the box and put the signals against the train. Some mailbags are taken, following which the Mail continues on its journey.

Friday 3. Sir William Goulding places before his board a memorandum handed him by the President yesterday setting forth the Provisional Government's proposals to facilitate the prompt and economical execution of repairs, defining the responsibility for carrying them out and fixing the financial liabilities to be accepted by the Government.

An attempt is made to derail the North Wall goods, D&SER, at Killiney, Co Dublin. About 06.00 some twenty men armed with rifles and revolvers arrive at the station and proceed to remove granite coping stones from the overbridge at the Killiney side of White Rock, a popular bathing place. The stones are placed as an obstruction on the up line to Dublin and two lengths of rail raised. Some of the men go to the signal cabin and hold up the signalman, interrogating him as to when the goods is due. They order him to place the appropriate signal at danger. About 06.30 the goods, with about 40 wagons, approaches and the signalman is directed to allow it to run into the station but not beyond it. When the train stops the men remove the crew and order the guard to release the brakes. They then force the driver to restart the engine, the station staff are herded into the signal cabin and the train set off towards the obstruction. As it climbs a slight gradient it is observed by milesman Patrick O'Toole who is coming in the opposite direction, having been walking the line. He had come across the stones and with the aid of a flashlamp discovered that fishplates holding the rails to the sleepers had been removed. 'I immediately hurried to the station', he says, 'in order to meet the goods train, but before I reached it I saw what I took to be the goods train approaching me. I showed the red light and stood in the centre of the line waiting for the train to pull up. It showed no signs of slackening and when it was almost abreast of me I noticed that it had no wagons or driver. It passed me at a rather slow rate. I dropped my lamp and coat and boarded the footplate. In doing this I hurt my knee and remained clinging to the cab rails of the engine for a few seconds. Using all my strength I pulled myself onto the footplate and managed to shut off the steam.' The loco halted within some 30 metres of the obstruction. Had the engine been derailed, says O'Toole, it would probably have been hurled across the railway embankment into the sea. Milesman O'Toole is granted a bonus, amount not stated, 'as a reward for the commendable effort he made in stopping the engine that was in motion and uncontrolled'.

On the GS&WR, Sallins Junction, Co. Kildare is raided at about 01.00. When the news reaches Naas, some 3 km distant, a Free State cycle patrol of 12 soldiers sets out for the station where it is fired upon and Volunteer Crampton, Naas, fatally wounded in the first volley. Military HQ, Railway Hotel, Galway reports that all bridges between Athenry and Tuam were blown up last Thursday night. The signal cabin at Ballyglunin was burned to the ground.

On the D&SER the evening Waterford–Dublin mail train is held up at a steep embankment near Glenmore station. Twelve armed men, who order passengers to remain in their seats and not look out the windows, enter the guard's van and painstakingly search the parcels. They are apparently looking for articles of clothing, expecting to find a large consignment of wearing apparel and bicycles from Waterford firms. The search lasts nearly an hour, after which some bicycles and parcels are removed and the train allowed to proceed. It reaches Westland Row, Dublin two hours behind schedule.

Saturday 4. The strike continues. Further to the events of Wednesday last the GS&WR advises that it has arranged for Dublin traffic to be dealt with at Sallins station as there will be large quantities of traffic remaining there overnight. They ask that a military guard should be supplied for the station. Pickets at Naas prevent traffic from Dublin by road being admitted to the station for onward dispatch by rail. The company had announced a regular goods service between Naas and Limerick with onward connections, but the picketing extends to Sallins and the projected goods service is suspended.

Sleepers, mile posts and stones are placed on the line from the 78¾ to the 79¼ milepost between Waterford and Campile on the Rosslare line. A notice posted at the 79 milepost reads: NO INTERERENCE BY CIVILIANS WILL BE TOLERATED and another at the 79¼ mile post: TRAITORS BEWARE. DEATH PENALTY . THIS SECTION IS MINED. The obstacles are removed and the train service resumes the same day. On the Cork & Muskerry a train is held up at Hayfield Crossing by armed men and the mailbags taken away. On arrival of the 09.15 at Donoughmore armed men enter the station and also remove mailbags.

Sunday 5. Grace Dieu signal cabin, on the southern side of the Suir at Waterford, is burnt. [Grace Dieu was the junction for Waterford South station, the terminus of the line from Limerick from 1878 until the river was bridged in 1906. Waterford South was used by the firm of Waterford Ironfounders until 1974. It closed completely two years later].

Monday 6. Drumcondra signal cabin, Dublin, is completely destroyed. [Drumcondra station was opened by the MGWR in 1901, closed in 1910 and re-opened as a suburban station on the Arrow network in 1998].

Tuesday 7. At Liffey Junction, Dublin where the GS&WR and MGWR lines converge, a large engine of the latter company, *Avonmore*, is detached from an arriving cattle train by armed raiders who apparently had originally intended to destroy the station, and set in motion. It runs at high speed, estimated at close to 100 km/h, to North Wall where it collides with and destroys seven wagons. The points are, fortunately, so made as to direct the loco into the London & North Western yard – had it entered that of the Midland Great Western the crash would almost certainly have detonated six barrels of gunpowder recently arrived and awaiting shipment to a Midland town.

According to the GS&WR General Manager E. A. Neale the military from time to time place a number of armed men on the footplate of engines for the protection of the train; but that arrangement, he says, is very inconvenient to the drivers and firemen and he is taking it up with the military authorities. There is shooting near Grand Canal Street engine shed on the D&SER. Men are searched by a number of Free State troops, the officer in charge of whom is under the influence of drink.

The engine and 11 wagons of the Limerick goods is derailed midway between Portlaoise and Portarlington on the GS&WR. Fireman William Dwyer is instructed to return to Portlaoise to report the matter to the railway and military authorities. He is arrested by the latter on suspicion of being implicated in the derailment. Dwyer will be released on 16 December having signed the customary form of undertaking not to use arms against the Government, not to support in any way such action and not to interfere with the property and persons of others.

Wednesday 8. Report no. 199. Ministry of Industry & Commerce (Transport Dept.), 14 St Stephen's Green: the 07.20 GS&WR train from Cork to Mallow which is being worked by pilot is stopped at Kilbarry by armed men who remove the train crew from the engine and order all passengers to alight. The engine is uncoupled and run up against the coaches sending them back into the tunnel. It is then put across the up line at Kilbarry and started for Monard Bridge where it collides with a van in the rear of coaches forming a military post. Six soldiers are reported injured. On the Killarney branch, milesman P. Flynn is held up by armed men and the letters addressed to the Permanent Way Inspectors in the Kerry district taken from him. The men tell him they will send on the letters themselves. An engine is taken off a goods train at Streamstown on the Midland Great Western and started down the line. It runs as far as Athlone where it is stopped without doing any damage.

A General Financial Report, dated and signed by Col. Russell, states that 'The organisation now known as the Railway Protection, Repair & Maintenance Corps owes its existence directly to: a) the economic situation brought about by the extensive unemployment in the ranks of railway workers as a result of the destruction of considerable sections of the railway system throughout Southern Ireland and b) the need of some organisation capable of carrying out repairs to the permanent way in Hostile areas where it was found impracticable for the railway authorities to proceed with the work of repair in the ordinary way, and the necessity of some arrangement to combine repair, protection and maintenance with the object of keeping open at least a minimum railway service in the interests of the public and the State. As a result of these circumstances instructions were given for the immediate formation of the Corps'. Its strength is not to exceed 2000 to 31 March 1923. Its structure is detailed as follows:

Organisation
In the formation of this Corps it must be borne in mind that the business of establishing such a unit occasioned from the beginning the outstanding difficulty of having to organise and at the same time carry on the functions for which the Corps had been set up.

Existing Commands
Thurles. One Company & Armoured Train no.1. 8 officers, 271 other ranks.
Cork. Two Companies and Armoured Train no.3. 9 officers and 348 other ranks.
Limerick. One Company & Armoured Train no 2. 2 officers and 61 other ranks.
H/Q Training Company established at Baldonnel. Chiefly for musketry instruction. H/Q at Portobello. Totals 42 officers, 939 other ranks.

Operations
The first Command to be established was organised at Thurles at the end of the month of September. This Command at once set about carrying out repairs to the Thurles-Clonmel line with the result that the line was open for traffic within three weeks from the date on which the first detachment of the Corps arrived on the area. On completion of actual repair work on this section of the line, work was immediately undertaken on the Clonmel-Waterford line which was reported fit for traffic on 5 October.

Blockhouses

Small corrigated [*sic*] iron hut built in five completed sections with an encircling defensive wall of sandbags. The first near Fethard. Lancias equipped with Lewis guns.

Hostile Action

Mostly that of small parties opening fire on working gangs and detached posts, with the exception of one incident in the Cork Command when a man from one of the posts wandered away from his comrades and was killed, the results of these attacks have been inconsequential.

The first railed Lancia was used on night patrol on the Thurles–Clonmel shortly after the line had been repaired for traffic. 'One night a large party of Irregulars (estimated at about 200-300 strong) attacked the car at a place named Moyglass, between Lafffansbridge and Fethard, the line having been mined in front and rear and at the same time heavy machine gun and rifle fire being opened upon it. The crew of the car put up a stubborn fight lasting 4 hours when they were obliged to surrender owing to the lack of ammunition, taking care to render useless their machine gun and rifles. All the crew with the exception of the Officer in Charge were wounded but not seriously. The car was not badly damaged...the attackers made prisoners of this crew but released them within a few hours.' [See 15 October 1922].

Thursday 9. The General Manager of the Cork Bandon & South Coast, John R. Kerr, reports that Messrs Skelton & Co. have sent over some men and material from Britain in connection with the restoration of Chetwynd viaduct and that he will arrange with the military authorities for protection of the work.

The destruction of railway bridges and rolling stock and the burning of signal cabins has, in the view of today's *Irish Independent*, 'become so common of late that the plain people now accept these tactics as part of the campaign directed against the Government which the people themselves have placed in power...notwithstanding this deplorable condition of things the opponents of the Government have now had recourse to even more deadly methods. Yesterday a passenger train between Cork and Mallow was subjected to machine gun and rifle fire...'

Friday 10. Paddington station, London. The board of the Fishguard & Rosslare Railways & Harbours Company hears a report from the GS&WR giving details of the sections of railway which are at present closed to traffic owing to the action of Irregular forces. Amongst these is the line from Rosslare to Waterford, and it is suggested that if the Fishguard Company so desire the D&SER are willing to afford them access to the latter place by permitting GS&WR trains to run to Waterford via New Ross. After considering the position, however, the Board decides that the circumstances do not warrant advantage being taken of the D&SER's offer at the present time.

[The explanation of this confusingly worded report lies in the fact that the cumbersomely titled FRRHC existed as a holding company only, jointly owned by the Great Western Railway of England and the GS&WR. Formed at the close of the nineteenth century specifically to develop the two ports and build a railway carrying traffic through Rosslare to Waterford and beyond, its steamer and rail service was inaugurated in August 1906]. As the GS&WR strike continues a service is being maintained between Kildare and Buttevant.

Saturday 11. On the MGWR, a special train from Claremorris to Ballina is stopped at Balla. The engine and some wagons are detached and sent down the line towards Manulla Junction. They come to a halt in the section and the wagons are taken off and the engine sent under full steam down the line. It runs into a siding and stops, obviating a collision with a passenger train which is standing at the station.

At about 05.00 on the Wexford side of Killurin station on the D&SER the rails are broken ahead of the night goods from Dublin, hauled by loco no. 18 *Enniscorthy*, a powerful 4-4-0 built in Grand Canal Street works in 1910. The raiders stop the train by signal and take off the crew before wrecking the engine, which rolls over and over down the bank ending up on its side in the river Slaney. A breakdown gang arrives at 07.30 and the road is deflected round the wrecked train and reopened by 09.00. The locomotive is subsequently rescued by laying a temporary line along the shore an up onto the Slaney bridge and along the county road to the railway embankment.

Monday 13. The first pig fair for a considerable time is held in Clifden, Co. Galway. The pigs bought have to be driven on foot – or trotter – to Oughterard, the nearest open station. In the absence of rail services and with sea connections suspended during the winter the people of Clifden are, it is said, 'faced with starvation'.

Tuesday 14. The enrolment of 2000 men in the Railway Corps is approved by the Government. Again on the D&SER, the 19.55 train from Macmine is boarded at Rathgarogue station by about 12 men who uncouple the engine and order the driver to set it in motion, with the result that about 3 km further it is badly derailed. The line will reopen for traffic on the 17th.

The 18.15 Limerick–Nenagh is held up between Castleconnell and Lisnagry. Driver John Crossan, Nenagh and fireman William Nolan, Limerick are ordered out and the train sprinkled with petrol and set on fire. Crossan is then compelled to restart the locomotive which, with the burning train attached, travels as far as Castleconnell where it comes to a halt on a rising gradient. The fire, confined to the leading coach of five next to the engine, is extinguished and the remaining vehicles are undamaged.

Wednesday 15. From Commandant Adjutant, Western Command, Athlone to Military Secretary to C-in-C: 'It is feared that for the present at least adequate protection cannot be afforded to those premises [Mallaranny Hotel] as this District is infested by roving bands of Irregulars.' In Dublin, armed men raid the Donnybrook depot of the Dublin United Tramway Co.

Thursday 16. Killala signal box, MGWR, is burned down. Practically all the wires on the system are cut and the company cannot obtain information. There is a raid on the goods store at Aghada on the Cork Blackrock & Passage. The Dublin United Tramway Co. successfully bids £8000 bid for the premises of the Sackville Street Club, intended for its new head office.

Friday 17. Representatives of the GS&WR meet with the Minister for Industry & Commerce to discuss the position of the railways after 6 December next, when the Free State officially comes into existence. The company's permission to Cork drivers to borrow from the Enginmen's Fund is extended to Inchicore, Waterford, Limerick and Tralee. A letter is received from the above Minister submitting amended proposals with regard to compensation for malicious damage to the railways. It is learned that Free State forces are proposing to occupy the Waterville Hotel.

The reduction of staff and transfer of officials resulting from the introduction by the D&SER of a cheaper and accelerated service between Dublin Westland Row and Greystones is causing unrest amongst employees.

Saturday 18. A bomb is thrown at a DUTC tramcar passing ruined buildings on Ormond Quay. Two passengers are slightly wounded.

Monday 20. A GS&WR special runs into a wall of stones built across the line between Farranaleen and Fethard, the engine being damaged. The first of two new West Clare engines, 4-6-0T no. 3 *Ennistymon*, arrives at Ennis. The Bray goods is held up at Foxrock, Co. Dublin, the raiders removing whiskey – and Oxo.

At Sparrowsland siding on the D&SER line between Palace East and Macmine Junction the Waterford goods is held up by armed men who, having stopped the train by waving lamps and placing fog signals on the track, break it and pull the rails to the edge of the bank. The locomotive, 0-6-0 no. 36 *Wexford*, is uncoupled and run off into marshy land, landing with her wheels in the air. The engine is later salvaged and returned to duty and the undamaged wagons retrieved. The purpose of this attack is not clear. [Virtually no visible evidence now remains of this unpeopled line, opened in 1887, never profitable and closed completely through to New Ross in 1963].

80

Tuesday 21. Most of the MGWR system is now functioning with the exception of the Westport–Achill, Oughterard–Clifden and Manulla–Killala sections. An unsuccessful attempt is made to wreck the D&SER 05.40 goods at Foxrock, Co. Dublin: a bonus of £5 is awarded to guard Donoghue for his role in the attack. The GNR reports 29 cases of interference since 7 November. The Provisional Government disclaims any rights or responsibilities with regard to the railways in the Northern (Six Counties) area.

Thursday 23. Mr Kerr, stationmaster at Crossdoney, the junction for Killeshandra on the MGWR, receives a communication from the Irish Republican Army [Irregulars]: 'Take notice you are to have Mrs & Miss Birrell, Level Crossing Leggaginey, removed from the Company's House at said Crossing within 10 days from above as they are a menace to the movements of Republican Troops. Failure to comply with above will incur drastic action. GHQ Army Executive.' Leggaginney is south of Crossdoney on the line to Inny Junction. [This line, from Inny Junction to Cavan via Crossdoney, was opened in 1856 and closed completely in 1960. The branch to Killeshandra opened in 1886 and was closed to goods in 1944 and to all traffic in 1955].

The board of the Cork Bandon & South Coast decides that provisional notice be given to the chief officers that after 31 December their salaries will, while the line remains closed, be paid at only three-fourths of the present rates. The services of agents and clerical staff still employed are to be dispensed with after 1 January 1923: they are to be offered re-employment as caretakers at two-thirds salary. Agents living in the company's houses are to be subject to a nominal rent of one penny per week, pensions not being affected. Walking [by milesmen] of the permanent way is to be reduced to three days per week. The line remains closed.

Friday 24. The bridge between Cahir and Clonmel on the GS&WR, to which temporary repairs enabling the train service to be resumed have just been carried out, is again blown up at about 10.00. The Permanent Way Inspector and his men are working here when over a hundred armed men arrive and place them under arrest, after which they proceed to blow up the bridge with mines. They stop the 08.50 passenger train from Limerick some distance from the bridge, order the passengers and train crew off, and send the train at high speed into the damaged bridge resulting in the engine and carriages being badly damaged and derailed, the engine being thrown down the slope. When the Railway Corps armoured train reaches the place in the evening it is found that the coaches have been completely burned, the raiders, it appears, having returned in lorries for this purpose.

A meeting of the Chairmen and General Managers of the railways of 'Southern Ireland' is held in the Railway Clearing House, Kildare Street, Dublin. Sir William Goulding is in the chair. All except the D&SER representatives, who are neutral, are against the proposed unification. It is resolved that 'the Railway Companies undertake to prepare a scheme or schemes for Grouping as soon as possible, and to report the result within six months from 1 January 1923'. All present are in favour of grouping except the D&SER, Dublin & Blessington, Cork & Macroom, Cork Blackrock & Passage, Cavan & Leitrim and the Waterford & Tramore who reserve their position.

Under the heading RAILWAY FACILITIES (?) the *Waterford News* comments that 'the Dublin & South-Eastern train timed to arrive in Waterford at 10.50 pm has been reaching the city of late at all kinds of unearthly hours. Invariably her time of arrival has been about 1 am whilst on one occasion during the present week the train did not reach Waterford until 5 am. The times we live in may, we suppose, to a large extent be responsible for the repeated delays'. The Waterford station signal cabin, with 64 levers one of the most important on the GS&W system and carried on a gantry over the tracks, is completely destroyed by fire.

Saturday 25. From T. MacHale, District Inspector, Longford to the MGWR head office: 'The attached note was handed to me today by two strange men, who stated that if Mrs Birrell and daughter were not removed from Leggaginey Crossing withn 10 days, the house, etc. would be destroyed. Please note and instruct. Yours obediently, H. Kerr.'

The 16.00 train ex Ennis on the West Clare is held up at Cloonadrum cutting, beyond Kilmurry, by armed men who, having removed the passengers and parcels, order the driver to put on steam and to run 100 yards and then to leave the engine. Before doing so, however, he puts on the injector and opens the regulator, thus preventing greater damage as the engine immediately runs into a barricade of stones on Annageragh bridge, lifting the bogie and front driving wheels off the rails. Driver Cosgrove, fireman O'Donoghue and milesman M. McDonnell – and the Road Inspector – are specially commended for their loyal work in connection with the outrage. A bonus of £2.10.0 is 'granted in the special circumstances and is not to form a precedent'. On the D&SER engine no.36, 0-6-0 *Wexford*, built 1900, [see 20 November] is derailed at milepost 85 by the removal of rails. The line is badly damaged and the engine overturned.

Sunday 26. Foxrock signal cabin, Co. Dublin, is burned to the ground by armed men.

Tuesday 28. A second meeting to consider unification with Sir William Goulding again in the chair. Gordon Campbell, on behalf of the Minister of Industry & Commerce, expresses his regret for the absence through illness of the Minister, Joseph McGrath. He states that in the opinion of the Government some change in the existing administration of railways in Ireland is absolutely necessary, and the Government had hoped that the companies with their experts would have come to its assistance formulating a scheme or schemes for grouping. If such a scheme were to be formulated by the Government, which had no officials capable of handling such a question, it was just possible that something might be forced upon the railways that would be almost unworkable and cause endless confusion and additional expense.

Introducing the estimate on the railways in the Dáil, President Cosgrave says of the Dublin & Blessington: 'the railway is an unfortunate one. The part of the railway in Co. Wicklow is expensive. It is expensive because of the very irregular level, and the line has many twists and turns which make it very expensive to run. I understand that it would be possibly line ball if it were to run from Dublin to Tallaght'.

On the D&SER armed men make another unsuccessful attempt to derail a passenger train (one of the new 'saloon trains' of open-plan coaches) at Dalkey at 23.00. The driver, fireman and passengers are ordered off and the former then compelled to set the train in motion. He remains on the footplate until the loco runs into coping stones placed on the track, damaging but not derailing the engine. The passengers left at Dalkey station have to make their own way to their destinations: some are courteously accompanied by one or other of the raiders.

Wednesday 29. An unaddressed, unsigned and undated letter is received by Mr Nihan, stationmaster, Blanchardstown, on the MGWR. It states that 'information has been received here, that you have been using your influence with the Midland Great Western Railway to put a siding at Blanchardstown for the purpose of carrying the traffic of the British Margarine Company, if this is carried into effect it will mean the throwing of 6 to 8 men out of work that most of whom have large families to support. As the state of the country do [sic] not permit more unemployment and starvation we, the Soviet Party of Ireland, warn you that unless you withdraw your proposals at once you and your friend will suffer the extreme penalty. Signed THE SOVIET PARTY'. The traffic of the company is presently being carried by road. In the Dáil a captured document is read containing instructions for the general destruction of communications, particularly of railways.

Thursday 30. The CB&SCR Works in Cork have been closed during the past week. Crossing keepers are leaving their houses to obtain work, the gates are open and cattle continually grazing on the line. The Board of Directors of the D&SER state that they 'fully recognise the importance of placing the railways of Ireland in the most satisfactory position possible in the general interests of the country, and as it is understood that the other railways of Ireland have expressed the view that this position will best be assured by some system of Grouping, the D&SER Co., while not accepting that view, are prepared to acquiesce in the principle of Grouping, but in the absence of further information, they are not prepared to commit themselves to any particular Grouping scheme'. A conference, in the Shelbourne Hotel, Dublin, involving railway managers and representatives of the National Union of Railwaymen to consider wages and conditions is adjourned to 8 December.

On the GS&WR the four-coach 07.30 Cork–Dublin train is held up between Rathduff and Mourne Abbey and the crew and passengers ordered off. The last coach is set on fire and the train restarted at speed, running for about 3 km with the carriage burning fiercely. Eventually the vacuum brake catches fire, bringing the train to a standstill. A Railway Corps armoured train is quickly on the scene and the damaged train is driven without incident to Mallow. The service out of Cork resumes with the 13.15 but passengers are obliged to walk from the scene of the incident to Mourne Abbey, from were they are taken in a fleet of motor cars to Mallow.

The 11.55 goods ex Maryborough [Portlaoise], hauled by 101 class 0-6-0 no. 254, is derailed together with her tender and six wagons. [The locomotive, built in 1903, is retrieved and is to survive in service until 1961].

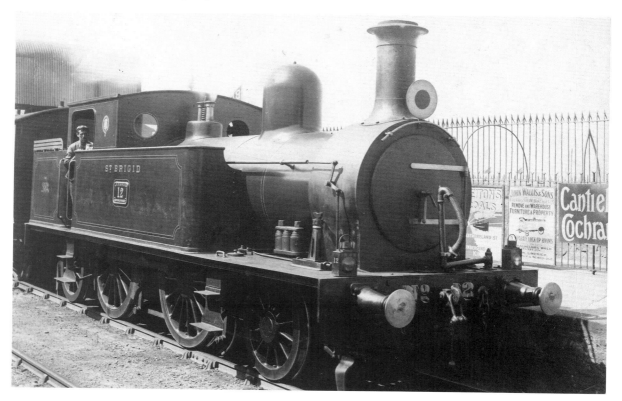

D&SER 2-4-2t No. 12 *St Brigid*.

A MAN WITH A HOSE

Friday 1. The position of the railways in view of the coming termination of the Agreement with the Government on 31 December is seriously engaging their managements. Suggestions are being made for a State subsidy until normal conditions are restored to guarantee a reasonable dividend to shareholders. Earnings, according to the companies, are not paying the working expenses and without State aid, they say, even a curtailed service could not be maintained.

Saturday 2. Work is to be proceeded with on a plan for goods and cattle accommodation at the temporary GS&WR station at Mallow South, in use since the Blackwater viaduct was destroyed. On the West Clare 20 or 30 men raid Doonbeg goods store and take away one chest of tea, consigned to Mrs Ryan, Cree, who has been duly advised of its arrival, and should have had it removed.

Monday 4. A shooting incident at Harcourt Street, Dublin results in the wounding of two passengers on the Dartry Road tramcar no. 202. [Route 14, opened 27 January 1905, closed 31 October 1948]. The GS&WR says it is not anxious to work the line between Rosslare and Waterford until protection asked for the Barrow bridge is given.

Wednesday 6. Saorstát Éireann, the Irish Free State, comes into being today and issues its first postage stamp, bearing a white map of Ireland on a green ground. The 15.35 GNR goods ex Dublin is boarded whilst in motion a short distance north of Mountpleasant, between Dundalk and Goraghwood on the Belfast line, and six barrels of porter removed. No political significance is attached to the incident. A telegram from the Portarlington stationmaster informs the GS&WR management that a runaway engine passed that station at 23.03 last night. A livestock special had left Portarlington at 20.55 and the unmanned locomotive ran into the brake van of the special. The guard succeeded in holding it and taking it to Cherryville Junction. Another report is received to the effect that the viaduct over the River Nore at Thomastown was burnt down last night, 12 metres of both waybeams in the centre of the structure being destroyed.

Thursday 7. The Government gives the railway companies six months from 1 January 1923 'to bring forward a scheme or schemes of grouping'. They are to discuss wages and conditions with the trade unions but if there is no settlement the Government will deal with the matter itself. Under no circumstances, it intimates, can it allow a strike to take place. In the Dáil, P. Hughes

(Louth & Meath) asks Joseph McGrath, Minister for Industry & Commerce, 'if he is aware of the serious inconvenience and loss caused by the continued stoppage of the railway service between Dundalk and Greenore, owing to a damaged bridge'. The Minister replies that the Ballymascanlon viaduct on the Dundalk Newry & Greenore Railway between Dundalk and Greenore had been blown up some time ago. It was repaired by the company but again blown up within ten days of being repaired. 'Up to the present the Company did not consider it prudent to further repair the viaduct...I have learned since I came to the Dáil that the Engineer has been instructed to proceed with temporary repairs immediately'. [Owned by the London & North Western Railway, the DN&G was opened from Dundalk to Greenore in 1873 to service the new harbour and its ferry services to Holyhead and the Isle of Man. In 1948 it became the property of the nationalised British Transport Commission. The line from Greenore to Newry Bridge Street opened in 1876. Ballymascanlon viaduct was a 22 span iron girder bridge located some 1.5 km from Dundalk Quay Street station. The entire line was closed in 1952, having suffered economically, in common with the other cross-border railways, from the imposition of partition in 1920].

Sir Thomas Henry Grattan Esmonde, Chairman, Dublin & South Eastern Railway, is one of 30 people nominated to the new Senate by the President of the Executive Council, W. T. Cosgrave. John Bagwell, General Manager of the Great Northern, is similarly honoured [see 30 January 1923].

The Cork Blackrock & Passage line is still closed in its entirety, but the MGWR has authorised the opening of the Westport and Achill branch and trains were reintroduced on that section yesterday.

Friday 8. On the CB&SCR a train bringing workmen to repair the viaduct is fired at, but there are no casualties or damage. When another train is attacked on 15 December work stops and the erectors are sent back to England. The 08.15 train ex-Achill runs off the road after leaving Mallaranny owing to rails having been removed and after its brief reinstatement the line is once again blocked.

The 21.15 passenger train from Wexford to Waterford, hauled by engine no. 32, is held up at Macmine Junction. The raiders are intending to take D&SER 4-4-0 no.68 *Rathcoole* (one of the two largest express engines ever owned by the railway) off the 18.05 ex Harcourt Street which crossed the Wexford-Waterford at Macmine. Finding the not unsympathetic John 'Sketch' White on the footplate, however, they opt for no.32. They evacuate both passengers and crew who are destined to spend a cold and hungry night at the station, which is a railway junction only, without shops or other amenities. The raiders then take the train to Killurin where the loco is detached and sent into the river, joining no. 18 there. Both are to await rescue until after Christmas, when they are removed and eventually restored to service.

The Mayo Mail, MGWR, running as a special, is stopped in the evening at Liffey Junction to await the clearing of the platform at Broadstone, its destination. A group of armed men, whose intention was apparently was to burn the station, seize the opportunity and rush onto the platform, holding up the officials and taking the passengers out of the train, though several women and children are overlooked. The passengers are herded into a rear carriage while some of the vehicles next the engine are sprinkled with petrol and set on fire. The guard is ordered to uncouple the rear coach but before he can do so the train moves out. Some of the passengers manage to jump clear but three or four who are not able to do so reach Broadstone in a state of nervous collapse. The driver has succeeded in re-boarding the train after it was put in motion and, advance warning having reached the terminus, the points are set for a siding adjacent to the water tower into which he runs it and where the fire is extinguished. The women and children in the train are uninjured but Miss Munnelly of Ballina has her false teeth broken. Mr Cowell of the same town says he has been severely shaken by the experience.

Saturday 9. In Cork, the CB&SCR carriage and wagon shops are closed, and it is intended to close the fitting shops on the 23rd of the month.

Sunday 10. The D&SER Waterford goods store suffers a severe attack. The following day an unsigned Special Report is sent to Maj.-Gen. Joseph McGrath, Director of Intelligence, for forwarding to the Chief of Staff. It states that 'at about 10.10pm on last night (10.10.22) a Search Party under Capt. Cunningham and accompanied by the Assistant Intelligence Officer here was on the point of proceeding to Ferrybank to raid a 'Die-Hard' [Irregular] Dance when the Sentry on the tower of the jail here reported the railway station to be on fire. At the same time, a party from the Union, under Lieut. Tierney, was about to proceed to Ferrybank, but when fire was observed the Jail party proceeded at the double to the scene of the fire. The party from the Union came on the scene subsequently. When I arrived at the station, myself and Sergt. Power ran up to the engine shed, and got the only engine under steam. With this engine, we pulled out five train lengths of wagons, the majority of them loaded with goods. Some of the wagons had to be pulled out of the burning sheds, and it was only with great difficulty this was accomplished. Capt. Cunningham and myself, together with Sergt. Power and Sergt. Finnegan, endeavoured to get into the D.S.E. [Dublin & South Eastern] shed, which was blazing fiercely. We had to run an engine through the door to smash it in but, owing to the heat and the stifling fumes, we were absolutely unable to get out any more wagons. As a matter of fact, 5 or 6 of them were actually blazing at the time. Although the local Fire Brigade was 'phoned at 10.15pm, it did not put in an appearance at the scene until 11.45, although it was again 'phoned from the railway station. It arrived at the time stated, on a side car, and consisted of a man with a hose.

We did not get the fire under control until about 3 am on Monday morning, and during our exertions one Railway Clerk, the D.S. [District Superintendent] here, Mr Purdon and Inspector Scott were the only volunteers that came to our help, although the place where the fire occurred is full of railway workers. After the fire, we arrested the men as named on the enclosed list [*missing*]. They are all active Irregulars. 'Bunky' Cahill was arrested by me the night after the fire'. The GS&WR goods store housed 22 wagons, many containing foodstuffs; two carriages; one horse box and five ballast wagons. All were destroyed.

Monday 11. The majority report of the Northern Ireland Railway Commission recommends that the best method of working the railways is 'the continuance of the present well-established and competitive system of private management'. A minority report by Labour interests favours nationalisation.

Tuesday 12. A GNR goods is held up at Inniskeen by armed men who remove a large quantity of flour, sugar, tea and other commodities. Free State troops are rushed to the scene from Dundalk and Ballybay with the result that all the goods are recovered as they are being taken across the border. One man is arrested while engaged in removing items with a horse and cart.

Wednesday 13. M. F. Keogh, General Manager, Midland Great Western, presides by invitation as the College Historical Society, Trinity College Dublin, debates the motion 'that this House approves of the nationalisation of railways'. Responding to a vote of thanks he tells his audience that 'we railwaymen, thinking about this question of nationalisation, naturally view it from the angle of working conditions. You view it from a wider area – the question of how nationalisation would be likely to affect the community as a whole. I suggest that the question really is a simple one...would the railway system of the country be more efficient under a system of nationalisation than under commercial management?' He goes on to pose the rhetorical question 'who is it that most prominently urges nationalisation? The answer is – Labour'. Dealing with the problems resulting from partition Keogh says that 'unfortunately in this island we have two distinct Executives. The boundary, from the railway point of view, is impossible. It cuts through the Great Northern Railway, I believe, at 12 or 14 different places... if we are to have nationalisation, or grouping, which is an alternative, we ought to have it treating the railway system of Ireland as a whole, and there should be no attempt to truncate portions'.

33
Cahir, Co. Tipperary.
See 24 November 1922.

34
Destruction at Killaloe, Co. Clare.
See 18 May 1923.

35
Waiting for the 'School Train' at
Dripsey station, Co. Cork.
See 4 October 1922.

36 & 37

Palace East, Co. Wexford.
See 20 January 1923.
Two trains, the 06.30 goods
from Waterford hauled by loco
no. 61 and the 09.45 passenger
from Macmine Junction to
Waterford (loco no. 68) arrived
at the station shortly after 10.00.
They were seized by armed men
and set in motion towards one
another on the same track,
resulting in a head-on colision.
Both engines were beyond
repair and were scrapped.

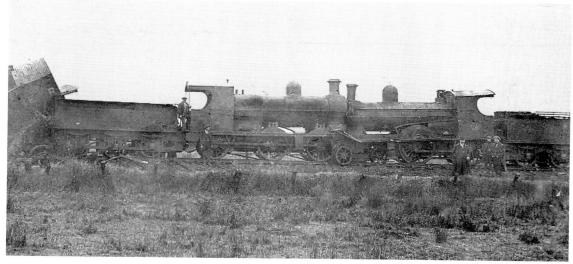

39
GS&WR hotel, Kenmare, Co. Kerry.
See 1 September 1922.

40
GS&WR hotel, Eyre Square, Galway.

41
Leenane hotel, MGWR.
See p. 148.

42
On the Timoleague & Courtmacsherry
Extension Light Railway.
See 15 August 1922.

43
Mallow South, Co. Cork.
See 9 August 1922.

44
Recovering loco no. 36, Killurin,
Co. Wexford, 14 October 1922.
Inspector Michael Forde is third
from right. The engine had left the
track following the removal of rails.

45
Nearly every loco on the MGWR was named. No. 126 *Atlantic* at Mullingar.

46
Ex GNR 4-4-0 *Blacklion* on the Sligo, Leitrim & Northern Counties at Manorhamilton. See 4 April 1922.

47
Charles Russell.
See 25 September 1922.

48
Railway Corps post.

Thursday 14. At a meeting of the railway companies at the Railway Clearing House, Dublin they are 'confirmed in their opinion that the formation of two Groups is preferable to unification, and that the best division is roughly North and South of a line drawn between Dublin and Galway'. On the MGWR between Kilfree and Ballymote the 12.10 passenger train is held up, the engine, no. 24 *Clifden*, detached and sent full steam to Sligo where it is derailed.

Friday 15. On the GS&WR Waterford Mallow line at Kilmeadan the 18.15 passenger train ex Durrow is fired on and stopped. The driver is compelled to propel the train back to the platform where the passengers are taken out, the train set on fire and started towards Waterford. The burning train reaches a point where a rail has been removed, derails and burns itself out, nothing remaining but the skeleton ironwork. As the passengers continue to Waterford on foot a Free State soldier amongst them is searched and his overcoat taken.

Saturday 16. The second section of the mail train from Dun Laoghaire to Westland Row is held up at Blackrock, Co. Dublin. A number of men who have been waiting for the train to arrive have forced the station staff into a room where they are held under armed guard. The signals are set against the train and the raid, in which three bags of mail are taken, is carried out so quickly that the passengers remain unaware of what it happening. The raiders escape by motor car.

Sunday 17. At 01.00 armed men call at the stationmaster's house some distance from Durrow station, Co. Waterford and compel him to hand over his keys. They then order him back to bed. On going to the station in the morning he finds the entire premises – booking office, waiting room, goods store and lamp room – gutted by fire.

Monday 18. A typewritten letter is received at Dundalk: 'From IRA HQ 2nd Battalion to T. F. Finegan, Stationmaster. 1. The Free State 'Government' are using the Railway for the transport of Troops and munitions in their attempt to destroy the I.R.A. and the honour of the nation. 2. I hereby give you warning that engine crews are liable to be fired on unless within 2 days I obtain from you a guarantee that the following will not be carried on trains in their area: a) Free State Troops whether armed or unarmed; b) Free State Intelligence Officers; c) Supplies for Free State Troops; d) Communications for Free State Troops. 3. The Railways will be protected if they are used only for ordinary traffic but the Free State 'Government' will not be allowed to use them for the furtherance of their present murderous war. (*signed*) O/C Battalion.'

The Minister for Industry & Commerce, Joseph McGrath, and representatives of the railway trade unions meet to discuss the proposals by the railway company managers for a variation in the national agreement. The Minister states that 'the Government, if committed to anything, is committed to unification rather than nationalisation'.

Tuesday 19. The D&SER General Manager, M. J. Maguire, finds it necessary to introduce restrictions to the Waterford Branch train service owing to the risks involved in running the trains, and to the 'falling off in the passenger traffic consequent upon the present political disturbances'. Armed men threatened to shoot Mr MacDonald, stationmaster at Rathgarogue on the Palace East-Waterford section, if he did not leave the premises within 24 hours. A clerk is now working the station. Taking note of 29 cases of interference since 6 December 1922, the GNR decides that it will not ask for any subsidy to enable it to carry on, if offered by the Free State Government. In the event of any announcement being made as to the control of the company, a strong protest will be at once lodged with the Free State and Imperial Governments.

Knead's Bridge over the Royal Canal between Lucan and Mullingar on the MGWR is blown up.

Wednesday 20. A group of 12 armed men, who are not disguised, take possession of Castlebellingham station on the GNR main line. They collect the station staff, including the signalman, and force them into the stationmaster's office, placing a guard. The telephone, telegraph and staff instruments are rendered inoperative. One man goes to the signal cabin and puts the signals against the 17.30 Limited Mail from Belfast which stops and is then boarded, the passengers being taken out. The train is then reversed onto the down line, set on fire and derailed, heavy Christmas mails being destroyed. The wreck is well planned, disclosing a thorough knowledge on the part of the raiders of points and signals and railway working generally. The passengers, numbering some hundred, are compelled to leave their luggage on the train to be subsequently burned. All are to spend six hours on the inhospitable Castlebellingham platform awaiting the arrival of a relief train. Meanwhile the wrecked train is approached by a slow goods carrying military stores and with an escort of 11 Free State soldiers which collides with the wrecked express. There are no injuries but the derailed train suffers extensive damage, three coaches, including the dining car, being completely burned out. The line is blocked but it is hoped to have it cleared by midday tomorrow.

The Dublin & Wicklow Manure Co. has given notice that it will suspend work at its factory at Ballybough at the end of this week owing to the disruption of rail transport. Unless there is a speedy improvement in railway facilities it is feared that other Dublin factories may have to follow the same course.

In the Dáil, William Davin (Laois-Offaly) states that 'what I gathered from the negotiations that I took part in, during the last week or fortnight, was that certain railway companies or the directors of a particular railway, have informed the Government that they are not prepared to carry on the work of the railway after January the first'.

Thursday 21. In Crookhaven harbour, Cork, the Cork Bandon & South Coast steamer *Lady Isis* is fired on and one man, Able Seaman Shea, is wounded and cargo seized. The Dublin & Blessington train ex Terenure is held up at Brittas and all mails for Brittas, Manor Kilbride, Tinode and Blessington are taken away.

The President of the Executive Council, L T MacCosgair [W. T. Cosgrave] writes to Richard Mulcahy, C-in-C: 'Mr Bagwell [General Manager] of the GNR interviewed me this morning with reference to the outrages on his line last night. He gave me the attached short statement showing that out of the 80 attacks between October 1st and December 21st, 54 occurred in a very small area. Their total mileage is 562 miles and 67% of the outrages took place on 9% of the mileage. Another point of view he put to me was this. People have got more or less accustomed to outrages happening in the South of Ireland, but when they occur up towards the North they reflect more discredit on us than if they happened down South, and the nearer they get to the Northern Border the more dangerous they will be to any policy of reproachment and harmony which we may desire to pursue towards the North-East. His company were thinking of stopping the running of all passenger trains in the dark, but they have decided that the better course is to carry on... [*handwritten*]: Mr Bagwell is regarded as the last Unionist in Ireland and he has entered into the spirit of the change as a member of the Senate.' [See 30 January 1923].

Friday 22. The MGWR has received the authority from the local military officer to re-open the Galway–Clifden Line and expects to run trains tomorrow morning. A small group of Irregulars attacks Drogheda railway station.

Saturday 23. On the MGWR a ballast train is held up at Kiltoom, 8 km on the Roscommon side of Athlone. The crew is ordered off and the loco sent at speed towards Athlone. The stationmaster at Kiltoom succeeds in getting a message through by telephone and an engine and crew are made ready to block the progress of the runaway. As it approaches Athlone the manned engine runs at speed in front of it, gradually slackening pace until it makes contact with and succeeds in slowing the driverless engine, ultimately bringing it to a halt on the outskirts of the town.

Sunday 24. Christmas Eve. At a mass meeting of 300 railwaymen in Dublin a unanimous decision is made to reject the proposal by the MGW, GN and D&SER companies to introduce a flat rate reduction of 3s 6d weekly in wages. A similar decision is reached at meetings of three sections of the National Union of Railwaymen in Cork.

Thursday 28. All CB&SCR workshops are now closed but 15 men are employed on Government work.

Friday 29. The GS&WR is to ask Col. Russell to inform the company of the date of the inquiry into the damage to the stock shed at Inchicore on 22 December as the Board wish Mr J. R. Bazin, Chief Mechanical Engineer, to attend and 'give the Government every assistance in his power'. Liam Lynch, Director of Engineering for the Irregulars, emphasises the need for 'bringing Railways to a standstill, as on this to a great extent depends the success of our campaign'.

Free State troops operating from Waterford recover a quantity of looted beer on the premises of Mr Patrick Walsh at Cloggan. It is presumed that it is the beer which was taken during the raid on the 06.00 Waterford–Clonmel on Saturday last. It was found hidden in a haycock.

Sunday 31. The 17.05 train from Waterford to Durrow is derailed and the GS&WR orders that the line be closed until further notice.

D&SER 0-6-0 no. 17 *Wicklow*. See 10 July 1922.

IN TIME OF CIVIL WAR

SCALDED TO DEATH

Monday 1. Joseph Murphy, Stationmaster at Belmont & Cloghan on the GS&WR branch from Clara to Banagher, is obliged to leave when threatened by armed men and accused of being a Free State agent. [This 30 km line was opened in 1884, and as it provided access to the Shannon, was used in the latter part of the century and up until the 1914–18 war for excursion traffic which combined a river trip from Banagher to Killaloe with rail travel to and from Dublin. It closed to passengers in 1947 and to all traffic on 1 January 1963]. In the Dáil on 25 April W. Davin (Laois-Offaly) is to allege that 'the company was asked to follow the example of other Irish railway companies and to allow him [Joseph Murphy] his pay until such time as another position was found for him. This request was definitely refused, although the company was communicated with by the Minister for Industry & Commerce. The refusal was justified on the grounds of the financial position of the company. Just at this time substantial bonuses of from fifty to two hundred guineas were paid to some of the chief officials on the grounds of increased duties'.

A Midland Great Western goods train and two passenger coaches are set on fire at Kingscourt, Co. Cavan. Freelance criminal activity is suspected.

Wednesday 3. Raiders burn the temporary signal cabin at Macmine station together with the ticket office, waiting and refreshment rooms. The damage is estimated at £1400. Lieut.-Col. Tommy Ryan, in charge of operations in Wexford, later recalls that in January and February destruction was a daily occurrence, in spite of the presence of 950 Free State troops in the County. Kingscourt is again the subject of attack: three carriages are burnt and two locos damaged.

In the Dáil, in the course of an extensive statement on the future of the railways, the Minister for Industry & Commerce says that 'much thought has to be given to the question of how far the existing railways are really adapted to the needs of the country, how far they really serve the public interest, how far they are in parts comparatively useless, before the State agrees to purchase what might turn out to be in some respects a white elephant'. The Government's policy, he continues, 'is in brief to see that the present owners of the Irish railways bring the transport service for which they are responsible to the highest attainable degree of efficiency and economy. In the discussions in early December the companies were definitely informed that the policy favoured by the Government was the unification of the whole railway system under one management and the securing of the maximum economies in organisation and administration that unification rendered possible... the larger companies, on their part, represented that the objects desired by the Government would be better secured by a system of grouping than by complete unification'. The Minister suggests that the future of Irish railways has been uncertain since the ending of British-imposed control in August 1921. 'In the view that the country cannot allow the question to drift any longer, the companies have been informed that if they do not produce an agreed scheme of grouping such as the Government can approve within three months from 1 January 1923, legislation will be introduced with the object of bringing about unification within a period of six months from that date.'

The Government, he says, has concluded that it is necessary to maintain such services as are essential to the economic life of the community, 'and that where the company concerned is financially unable to do so the Government must find the money to enable those essential services to continue. But the cost to the State will be heavy'. Only those services which are really essential, he adds, would be maintained and any expenditure on permanent way or rolling stock that could reasonably be deferred would be prohibited for the time being. It is proposed to take this course in the case of the Great Southern & Western Railway. from the expiration of the notices [of closure on 8 January] which that company has issued. The policy which has been explained has primarily the circumstances in An Saorstát in view. There are obvious difficulties in securing an entirely satisfactory reform of the railway system unless it applies to the whole of Ireland, and it is sincerely to be hoped that that can be arranged by agreement amongst all parties. If, however, agreement proves unattainable, the Government is still concerned to see that the transport system of An Saorstát is efficient, and has no reason to anticipate that such difficulties as may be met with are likely to be insurmountable'.

Five companies are not at present running any trains: Cork Blackrock & Passage; Cork Bandon & South Coast; Cork & Muskerry; Schull & Skibbereen and Tralee & Dingle.

Thursday 4. Twelve Cork Bandon & South Coast employees are working on an armoured tank for the Government. Under the Irish Railways (Settlement of Claims) Act 1921 the amount awarded to the company is as follows:

Awarded by the Arbitration Tribunal	£75, 287. 0s. 0d
Interest	371 10s 10d
	75,658 11s 10d
Already paid	34, 804 17s 5d
Due	40, 853 13s 5d

With the Government pressing the company to expedite repairs, John R. Kerr, General Manager, writes to 'Col. Commndt. C.F. Russell, Commanding Railway Corps, Headquarters, Cork Command, GS&WR, Cork: In reply to yours of the 2nd inst. I can get men to work at Chetwynd Viaduct as soon as arrangements are made to convey them safely between Cork and the Viaduct. This will entail very efficient patrolling of the 5 miles of line concerned, and the provision of an armoured van and engine for the work, which latter would, of course, be available later for extended work. It would be necessary as a preliminary to the opening of the Bandon Company's line to properly protect the line say between Cork, Clonakilty and Dunmanway, including all the Bridges shown on the plan I sent you. The protection should be further extended to Bantry and Skibbereen as soon as practicable. When the above protection is effective, and subject to any further damage being done, I believe the Bandon Line can be opened for running in 3 to 4 weeks' time. I am, however, strongly opposed to any attempt to open the Line till effective protection can be given, as to do so will, I believe, only result in further useless destruction of works and rolling stock'.

The 05.00 Goods ex Dundalk is held up between Dundalk and Inniskeen on the GNR Cavan line. The crew are taken off and the train set ahead and derailed by a rail having been removed. Another GNR goods, the 07.15 ex Dublin, is held up by armed men at Killester Bridge, Clontarf. The engine is uncoupled, sent ahead and derailed. The 07.15 commuter service from Howth, coming in the opposite direction, fouls the derailed engine and several passengers are taken to hospital. At Clonmel the stationmaster receives a notice: 'Owing to the mean action of the enemy in continuing to travel in passenger trains together with the passengers in order to ensure their safety in moving from one area to another I am reluctantly compelled to issue instructions to have all passenger trains sniped in this area in future.' The notice is unsigned.

Joseph McGrath, Minister for Industry & Commerce, tells the Dáil that the President has received a letter from the chairman of the Great Southern & Western pointing out that, in view of the statement made here yesterday, his board has considered the matter very fully, and in view of the difficulties that might be placed in the way of all parties, that they have decided on carrying on from the 8th...they guarantee to pay the same wages as the other companies and carry on, as far as possible, as far as their financial resources will allow.

On the MGWR Meath branch armed men again attack Kingscourt station and sprinkle petrol on several carriages of the night passenger train from Dublin, setting them on fire. One third class carriage is completely destroyed and another, together with a first, damaged. The raiders then knock up a driver living some distance away, bring him to the station and compel him to set a standing goods train in motion, running it into a stationary engine. Both locos, no. 13 *Rapid* and no. 97 *Hibernia*, are derailed and badly damaged and the permanent way broken.

The 20 or so men involved remove a quantity of wine from the goods store before leaving. Some 4km away at Kilmainham Wood station they break into the goods store and come away with a supply of porter and groceries which they load onto a lorry commandeered from McEntee Bros. of Nobber. The men then make for the village of Kilmainham Wood where at 03.00 they break into the Post Office and smash the telephone apparatus. Their further operations are interrupted by the arrival of a party of Free State troops, but warned by a sentry the raiders break for open country after firing one volley. A running fight ensues over the fields but they make good their escape. The lorryload of goods is recovered. [Navan Junction to Kingscourt was opened in 1872/75 by the Navan & Kingscourt Railway. It closed to passengers in 1947. Goods services continued into the 1990s and the track remains in place though unused. Navan station, no longer a junction, remains open, handling mineral trains from Tara Mines to Dublin docks via Drogheda, but there is an aspiration to reconnect the town with Clonsilla and Dublin for commuter traffic].

Friday 5. Ennis station, where the narrow-gauge West Clare shares facilities with the GS&WR, is raided by armed men who compel the agent to hand over the sum of £30. 15s. 10d. The West Clare notifies the GS&WR that it holds it responsible, but the General Manager, E. A. Neale, replies on 30 January 'that his Company are including in their list of losses to the Government the cash taken from Ennis station...but beyond making the application it cannot accept any responsibility for the loss to this Company'. A letter from the 'Irish Republican Army' [Irregulars] to the stationmaster at Limerick Junction demands that he instruct all his drivers and firemen 'that from this date onwards they are to cease carrying Free State Troops, also Free State Intelligence Officers. Failing to comply with this Order all such men are liable to be shot at sight. (*Signed*) O/C 4th Battalion, 3rd Tipperary Brigade' (Seán Fitzpatrick, who describes his Brigade as 'a little Republic on its own'.)

John F. Sides, GS&WR Chief Engineer, Inchicore, writes to the Minister of Defence to the effect that a repair train has been held up about 2 km from Ballybrack station on the branch from Farranfore to Valentia in Co. Kerry. 'The working party were turned out of the train and an attempt made to run the train back to the broken bridge at the 44¼ mile post. The train, he says, did not, however, run very far, and the men got into it again and ran to Tralee. According to a letter from the District Superintendent's Office, Tralee: 'Driver was ordered to put it in motion and run it into the bridge. This he refused to do and one of the armed men then boarded the engine and started it away. It ran for about 600 yards and then very fortunately came to a stand, and before reaching the bridge. The gang of men was ordered to proceed to Ballybrack and this was being acted on – the driver and fireman remained and after about 15 minutes went after the engine which was then brought to Ballybrack.'

Saturday 6. In the early morning raiders hold up and derail a goods engine in a cutting at Raheny, on the GNR Dublin suburban line. The driver warns them that a passenger train from Howth is due and is allowed to take a red lamp and signal it to stop, but it strikes the derailed engine causing damage to itself and three of the train coaches. Some passengers suffer superficial injuries from flying glass. 'The worst I have yet experienced', says a Great Northern official, 'and one of the most marvellous escapes I have yet heard of. If the derailed engine had fouled the up line on which the Howth train was travelling by another 12 inches there would probably be 40 or 50 corpses lying here now.' Mr G Ellis, a postal official and a passenger on the Howth train, says he thought there was a heavy explosion rather than a collision. Superintendent Walker and a colleague are photographed partaking of an *al fresco* breakfast on a heap of debris on the tracks as the work of clearing the line proceeds.

On the D&SER the Palace East–Bagenalstown [Muine Bheag] train is held up, the raiders unhooking the engine and ordering the driver to wreck it by driving it over the track ahead, from which rails have been removed. The driver refuses, but one of the raiders, Peadar Sinnott, wrecks it for him. Two coaches and a van are burned.

Monday 8. 'Since August 1921', writes the *Irish Independent,* 'the obligations of the State to the railways are, in substance and justice, similar to those which had previously been undertaken by the British government. The Irish Railway Stockholders' Protection Association claim that the companies should be fully recouped for the losses due to abnormal conditions associated with the change of Government, and that upon the restoration of order they should be placed in as good a position as they were on the termination of British control. They point out that if the persons who provide the indispensable capital are not dealt with equitably confidence will be undermined, enterprise destroyed and credit shaken at the very moment when all the confidence, enterprise and courage of the people are needed to save the nation.'

Wednesday 10. Ganger Carton observes D&SER 2-4-0 loco no. 25 *Glenart* travelling minus its tender through New Ross. The stationmaster wires Inspector Forde in Wexford: 'No. 56 engine and carriages derailed Ballyanne. Van and 26 wagons pigs at Rathgaraogue. No. 25 gone through New Ross no tender nor no man. What about 26 wagons of pigs? Can anything be done?' No. 25 was assisting the 16.15 Enniscorthy–Waterford train and its engine, 4-4-0 no. 56 *Rathmines* when it was held up by at Rathgarogue by raiders who uncoupled the 26 wagons of pigs and left them there. The raiders then took no. 25 through the Ballintubber cutting and onto the Ballyanne embankment, planning to stage a run-back collision. The locomotive (driver Michael Hogan, fireman Thomas Lee) was held there in the dark for an hour or more, for unexplained reasons, and when the order was given by the raiders to move the locomotive further onto the bank steam was lacking. At this point a driverless no. 56 was hurtling down the track towards them. Both driver and fireman jumped clear and the impact of no. 56 on no. 25's tender, which it demolished, released the brakes on the latter loco and sent it off in the direction of New Ross, where it is observed by the astonished stationmaster. The runaway stops, having run out of steam, some distance out towards Glenmore. No.56 continues, pushing the remains of no. 25's tender, until she leaves the torn-up track and also comes to a halt. The following day both locomotives are recovered and subsequently returned to service, the pigs being hauled by two locomotives back to the passing loop at Palace East to allow the breakdown train through. They eventually reach Waterford, after which their fate is unrecorded.

On the MGWR a party of men raid Achill station and send three engines, nos. 14, *Racer;* 15, *Rover* and 35 *Airedale* at full steam in the direction of Mallaranny station. They are derailed at the 21¾ milepost through a rail being removed. The engines are damaged by sledge-hammers after being derailed and a train of empty carriages sent off the track. [The Westport to Achill branch opened in 1894/5 and lost its passenger service on 1 January 1935. It re-opened briefly in connection with road construction in the Achill area but closed again for good on 1 October 1937. The hotel at Malaranny [now Mulranny] and its station survives, though no longer in railway ownership].

Thursday 11. At 20.30 (Wednesday), an hour before curfew, parties of Irregulars enter Sligo town from different directions and launch a feint attack on the barracks, designed to keep the Free State garrison on the defensive whilst they wreck the station. At 23.30 a force of 40 armed men from the 1st Battalion of the 3rd Western Division, IRA [Irregulars] plant explosives there which detonate shortly after 02.00, destroying the offices and the accommodation of the stationmaster, Mr Hogg, which are completely burnt. When the containing force at the barracks withdraws troops arrive at the station but are too late to save anything – the military state that they tried to get the local fire brigade to turn out, but could not as the hose and other appliances were 'not available'. The roof girders fall in, completely blocking the permanent way. In the meantime an armed party enter the locomotive shed and hold the cleaning staff at gunpoint while they remove seven engines – five MGWR and two belonging to the Sligo Leitrim & Northern Counties. The three in steam are employed to move the coupled-up convoy out onto the running line where they are shunted in the Dublin direction to clear the points giving access to Sligo Quay, which is approached by a steep falling gradient. The points having been reset for the branch, the locomotives are started down the gradient where one smashes through the stop buffer into the deep water berth, another, no. 104, hanging over the harbour wall and the rest derailed and overturned. Twenty passenger coaches in the station are destroyed by fire together with four wagons. In spite of what the *Sligo Champion* describes as 'a scene of ruin and destruction that beggars belief' services resume the next morning to and from a point a short distance outside Sligo station, but the Free State garrison in the town is nevertheless criticised for its failure to respond to what will prove to be the single most destructive railway incident in the course of the war [see 15 January]. [The SL&NCR, which operated the line from Sligo to Enniskillen, had running rights over the MGWR from Collooney to Sligo, where it shared the facilities. In 1951 the company acquired 0-6-4T *Lough Erne*, which, with her sister *Lough Melvin*, became the last conventional steam locomotives to be delivered to any Irish railway. *Lough Erne* is in the care of the Railway Preservation Society of Ireland at its headquarters at Whitehead, Co Antrim].

Goods checker Joseph O'Connor is arrested at Portlaoise station.

Friday 12. The HQ of the Railway Protection Corps is transferred to Griffith [formerly Wellington] Barracks, Dublin from Baldonnel Aerodrome, Co. Dublin.

Saturday 13. There is an armed raid on the DUTC Sandymount depot. Precautions against a recurrence are to be taken. The company has moved to new premises at 59 Upper Sackville Street [subsequently O'Connell Street.].

There is an orgy of burning and destruction on the West Clare. At Corofin raiders announce that they are going to burn the station, but when Mr O'Sullivan, the stationmaster, remonstrates with them and asks are they going to burn the dwelling-house, they agree they will only burn the signal cabin. Nevertheless, all books, records and tickets and the flooring of two covered wagons are destroyed. Lahinch station is completely burned, and at Miltown Malbay the signal cabin is burned and an attempt made to burn the station, but the stationmaster, noticing the flames, comes down and extinguishes the fire with a bucket of water – the Manager, Robert King, proposes that he be commended for this. At Quilty all books, tickets, Post Office orders and stamps are destroyed; shortly after the raiders arrive the stationmaster's father dies of shock. All books, papers and tickets are also destroyed at Kilmurry, the staff being also taken and points injured. At Craggaknock and Doonbeg all the telephone instruments are taken. A number of telegraph poles are cut on the South Clare line (Miltown Malbay to Kilkee), rails removed at Clondrum and rails and sleepers taken between Monmore and Shragh siding.

A special of loco coal and empty wagons is derailed at bridge no. 78 on the MGWR near Streamstown. The two engines, no. 52 *Regent* and no. 135 *Arran Isles* are badly damaged, 14 wagons smashed and all the others badly derailed [see 16 January]. On the GS&WR a special, Limerick Junction–Mallow, is held up near the former station, the loco uncoupled, sent ahead to a point where the track has been lifted and derailed. A threatening notice is posted at the spot warning the per. way men that they will be shot on sight if they carry out repairs.

Some 200 passengers on the down evening Mail escape with their lives when between Lisduff and Templemore the train passes over a cattle culvert which has been blown up two minutes before, only the rails remaining suspended across the crater. The driver and fireman do not, however, hear the explosion and cross the gap at 70 km/h, both locomotive and carriages receiving a severe jolting, as a result of which the engine is badly damaged. The alarmed passengers are obliged to wait two hours for the arrival of a relief engine from Thurles.

Sunday 14. Malicious damage is caused to ten stations and signal cabins on the CB&SCR at Waterfall, Ballinhassig, Upton, Clonakilty Junction, Desert, Knockbue, Durrus Road, Bantry, Ballinascarthy and Clonakilty. Third Class carriage no. 33 is completely burnt and rails lifted near Ballymartle.

A GS&WR breakdown gang from Inchicore moving a derailed loco and repairing the per. way near Bagenalstown [Muine Bheag] is held up at 15.00 by armed men. Although threatened with being shot and having shots fired over him the driver refuses to start his engine, but the raiders succeed in setting it in motion. After proceeding for some 2 km it derails together with the large steam crane it is hauling. The attackers smash the crane's boiler mountings and gear wheel, setting fire to the train's stores wagon and brake van. Instructing the breakdown gang to leave the scene, the leader of the armed party tells them that the work of destruction will be continued for as long as Free State troops are moving by rail. The men have to walk through the fields for a considerable distance before reaching a village.

Monday 15. Armed men attack Free State troops who are in occupation of Dalkey station on the D&SER. Damage is slight. Raiders wreck the phone installation at Edermine Ferry on the D&SER. The Railway Protection Corps summarises the role of the Armoured Train and Lancia Car Patrols. 'The Command Armoured Train Engine and Fighting Wagons – in addition to being used for repair work are also used for patrol purposes. The train is sent out on a section to a certain point, the lights are turned out and the troops are taken out around the district searching houses, etc. etc. Other operations in connection with the armoured train consist of dropping troops along the line on an outward journey and picking them up on the return journey. The average distance troops move by this method is two miles.' The Lancia Car Patrols 'are used chiefly for the purpose of Company Commanders visiting their posts. Every post is visited by the C.C. at least once in every 24 hours'. The armoured trains are located as follows: no.1, Clonmel; no 2, Thurles; no. 3, Limerick; no. 4, 5 and 6, Cork; no. 7, Dublin; no. 8, Dundalk and no. 9, Mullingar. The trains consist of the armoured loco (partially-armoured in the case of no. 8) and one or two fully armoured cars or box wagons plus ancillary rolling-stock as required.

From Free State Army HQ, Sligo: 'A number of statements have appeared in the Press regarding the attack on the railway station on Wednesday night last which seem to have left the impression that the Army on that occasion did little or nothing to save the situation. The following facts, it is hoped, will help to correct this impression. The garrison of Sligo town all told numbered 70 effectives on the night in question, not 500, as appeared in a leading article of a Dublin paper. These had to guard a hundred prisoners, in the prison and three important posts in the town. Small parties of troops were out in the streets ten minutes after the first explosions were heard. One party reached the goods store in time to save it from destruction, and under heavy fire and without the aid of a fire hose or engine, saved an amount of rolling stock... Following the destruction a large number of arrests were made, including that of Christie McLynn, said to have been the driver of the armoured car *Ballinalee* after it was captured by an armed party in Co. Sligo.'

On the GS&WR, Mallow-Newmarket is re-opened, only to close again on 17 January. It is finally re-opened on the 25th. [The short Banteer-Newmarket branch was opened in 1889 by the Kanturk & Newmarket Railway. Closed in 1947 by CIÉ except for cattle specials and excursions, it lost all its services in 1963 and was lifted].

Tuesday 16. In Cork, 15 CB&SCR men are working on an armoured car for the military authorities, who have sent a body of men to the Albert Street terminus preliminary to taking steps for the re-opening of the line: Col. Russell writes that suitable arrangements have been made for protection and requests the company to proceed. The British contractors, Skelton, are to be asked to send over erectors again to work on the viaduct.

Near Streamstown on the MGWR workmen repairing the damage caused last Saturday are approached by unknown individuals who advise them that, if they would take a friendly hint, they will not be over-particular in the repair work, as it will shortly be undone again. At the same location the 20.20 Mullingar–Clara mixed train is held up and passengers and trainmen ordered off. The train is sent under full steam towards the engines and wagons previously derailed here last Saturday; its engine is now derailed there and the train partly wrecked. Both lines are blocked.

Over a hundred people, convoyed by the military, travel from Killarney to Tralee by road in search of food supplies. The journey is made necessary by the second failure of the train service. After a lapse of six months trains ran again for the first time on 8 and 9 January. On the night of the 9th, however, Currans bridge, only recently repaired, was again damaged with the result that the Gortatlea–Killarney section was again closed.

Final payment due to the D&SER under the Irish Railways (Settlement of Claims) Act 1921 amounts to £81, 648 2s. od. It would appear that Mr MacDonald, stationmaster, Rathgarogue, was threatened on account of his having notified Free State troops than an attack was about to be made at the railway station. An armed raid on the Dartry depot of the Dublin United Tramways at 23.30 proves ineffectual. [The Dartry route, no. 14, dated from January 1905. The attractive depot included an office occupied by an inspector and timekeeper and known locally as the Ticket Office. The line closed in October 1948].

Wednesday 17. Two armed men hold up one of the Listowel & Ballybunion engines a short distance outside Ballybunion station, compelling the driver and fireman to leave the footplate. They send the train under full steam into an open switch which is guarded by two other armed men. The engine leaps off the monorail and a metre down to the road where it is embedded in the gravel public by-way and badly wrecked. Two of the wagons are derailed and considerably damaged. The telephone has been taken down from the Post Office and the roads guarded to prevent the news reaching Listowel until a late hour. On leaving the place where the damage occurred the armed men state that they might return later to burn the premises.

Normal working is resumed on the West Clare, but a special to Kilrush is held up at Blackhills for about 45 minutes by old rails placed across the road and on the return journey this train and the 13.00 goods are held up at Miltown for about 90 minutes, as the milesmen who were removing the rails on a lorry report that they were called on from the hills to leave the scene. When they failed to do so quickly about a dozen shots were fired.

Thursday 18. In the CB&SCR workshops 18 men are employed plating an engine and van for the use of those repairing the Chetwynd viaduct.

The Rosslare Boat train, 18.05 ex Harcourt Street, with 4-4-0 loco no. 68 *Rathcoole* driven by John 'Sketch' White with fireman Jack Rogan, is ambushed at Scarawalsh between Ferns and Enniscorthy by armed men. Rails have been removed and there is no warning. The locomotive and two coaches leave the rails and driver and fireman clamber up onto the tender amid bursts of machine-gun fire. 'When we got off the engine', White later recalled, 'the man was there with the red lamp...I felt pretty hot and asked the man in charge – I didn't known him but he sounded like a West Cork man – what the so-and-so he though he was doing wrecking a passenger train without warning. He said we were running ahead of schedule – which we were not.' The women passengers are sent on to Enniscorthy in cars provided by the raiders but the men have to walk. Free State troops on board are deprived of their shirts and boots to provide disguises for the raiders, who then douse the coaches with petrol and set them alight, completely destroying new bogie coaches nos. 57 and 72 third class and no. 31 first class and 6-wheeled coach no. 19. The damage is estimated at £15,000. In the light of this incident the D&SER decide to run no more bogie coaches on their trains and reduce night running to a minimum. The breakdown crew arrive the following morning at 07.30 and succeed in getting the engine and wrecked coaches back onto the road.

A North Kerry Irregular unit led by Tom Driscoll of Kilmoyley attempts to derail a troop train at Liscahane bridge, no. 111, near Ardfert, lifting the rails and taking away a milesman as prisoner to prevent him warning the train on learning that it will be next on the line. The troop train, however, arrives late in Listowel and a goods train, the 08.15 ex Limerick, is sent to Tralee ahead of it. Driscoll, informed of the switch, has the signals set against the goods train at Ardfert and his men also fire shots in an attempt to stop it, but the train, travelling at 50 km/h, runs into the damaged bridge and the engine and 17 wagons are derailed, toppling down the embankment. The guard, John Glavin, frees himself from the brake van and crawls down to where the engine is lying on its side. He sees fireman Dan Crowley lying nearby calling out 'Save Paddy! Save Paddy!' He pulls him away from the loco which is belching steam and boiling water but fails in his attempt to extricate the driver, Paddy O'Rourke, from Tralee, who is dead and scalded beyond recognition. Aged 56, he leaves a widow and five young children. Fireman Crowley, 36, from Cork, dies later from his injuries. He was the sole support of his mother and a widowed sister and her five children.

Arriving two hours late for the Westmeath Agricultural Committee meeting at Mullingar the chairman, Canon Langan, PP, Moate, attributes the cause of his delay to the recent wrecking near Streamstown. 'I never witnessed such a terrible scene of destruction', he says. 'Amongst other features of the wretched scene is than of three wrecked engines, value each about £3000. How it went to my heart to see them lying there...I regret very deeply if Westmeath men should have a hand in this. People who destroy railway property are simply robbing widows and orphans. That is a sin that will cry to heaven for vengeance.'

Robert King, Manager of the West Clare, reports the receipt of a warning notice with reference to the usage of the company's railway by the military.

Friday 19. The 15.30 train on the Cork & Muskerry is held up between Firmount and Donoughmore by five armed men and one bag of mails removed. The GS&WR board orders that a report be sent to the Government concerning notices to stationmasters containing threats to drivers and firemen by Irregular forces. The General Manager enquires whether rent should be charged for premises, rolling stock etc. occupied by National troops. It is decided that rent be charged in all cases.

Saturday 20. At 03.00 the GNR viaduct between Malahide and Donabate north of Dublin is blown up, the explosion being heard in the city 15 km away. Damage to the up line is serious but the company succeeds in maintaining the service.

MGWR locos nos. 68 and 51 wrecked in a staged collision at Palace East.

Monday 22. At bridge 668 between Athlone and Kiltoom on the MGWR the down Mayo Mail is stopped and all passengers and the trainmen taken off. The train is then sent ahead into the bridge which is mined. Both engine and train are badly wrecked.

Tuesday 23. While engine drivers Dan Daly and Dan Lynch are chatting on the roadside outside Tralee railway station at 19.30 after shunting operations, two men wearing trench coats accost them. 'Are your Daly?' asked one. 'Are you Lynch?' queries the other. The drivers answer in the affirmative, whereupon the accosters draw revolvers and fire point blank. Daly dies; Lynch escapes with slight wounds. The killers are allegedly Free State officers.

Kilmessan station on the MGWR on the Clonsilla to Kingscourt line, junction for Athboy, is attacked, 15 armed men smashing the boiler and pumping plant. The stationmaster, Mr Foote, and his family are given ten minutes to leave and can only save two pictures and some clothes – all personal belongings, furniture, office equipment and instruments are destroyed. As a result trains are running late and engines have to take water at Dunboyne or Navan.

The Ballinrobe branch is closed in consequence of bridge 927 over the river Robe between Claremorris and Hollymount being blown. [The modest Claremorris–Ballinrobe branch, opened in 1892 by the Ballinrobe & Claremorris Light Railway, lost its service on 1 January 1960]. The MGWR chairman, Major Cusack, writes to Wm. Cosgrave Esq., President: 'Dear Sir. The Directors, at their Meeting today, have had before them the reports of the officers relative to the numerous recent cases of the destruction to Railway works and rolling stock, notably the serious occurrences at Sligo, in the neighbourhood of Streamstown, and on the Newport and Achill Section of the line. All cases of Malicious damage are reported to the Government from day to day through the Ministry of Industry & Commerce, and the officials of the Company are in close touch with the Military Authorities, to whom particulars have also been supplied. My colleagues and I realise fully the difficulties with which the Government is confronted in attempting to provide adequate protection for property throughout the disturbed areas in the Free State, and they appreciate very much the steps which have been taken by posting Guards at Broadstone, Liffey Junction and Sligo, as well as at some of the Passenger stations at Garrison towns. They would like to urge, however, that additional protection should be afforded at those points on the system where the consequences of interference would be most seriously felt. These points include, in the case of Railway works, the Leixlip Viaduct, the Shannon Bridge at Athlone, the Suck Bridge at Ballinasloe, and the Shannon bridge near Drumsna, and in the case of rolling stock, the several Depots where a considerable number of engines or of wagons are stored or have occasion to stand over night, as well as certain important stations and junctions. The question of providing a small Guard on important Main Line trains also is submitted for consideration. It is hoped that the Government will find it possible to afford additional protection against attack by evilly disposed persons, and it is needless to say that in such cases the Company will co-operate in every practicable way to secure that the steps taken may be effectual.' On the 30th the C-in-C writes a cover note to the Chief of Staff: 'Seeing that these facts have now been put in writing immediate action should be taken to prevent Irregulars destroying these places before we get a move on in the matter.'

The critical state of affairs is reflected in the MGWR's annual revision of salaries. Among the recommendations are:

Mr Seymour, Assistant Engineer. (£800 + £250). Since July last Mr Seymour has been almost continuously engaged in dealing with the repair of malicious damage to bridges and permanent way, frequently under conditions involving not only great discomfort but great personal risk. His action throughout has been of exceptional value to the Company directly, besides affording a most inspiring example to the men under him.

Mr Ffolliott, Acting Assistant Engineer. (£500 +£50). Mr Ffolliott has had charge of the organisation at headquarters under the Chief Engineer of the emergency work rendered necessary, including estimation and recording of damage, special safety precautions, dispatch of break-down gangs... He is responsible also for restoring navigation on the Canal when obstructed by the blowing up of bridges or otherwise'. [The Royal Canal is owned and operated by the MGWR].

Mr Murphy, Engineering Assistant: Bridges. Mr Murphy is responsible for designing the whole of the new bridge work maliciously destroyed...Mr Murphy prepares plans, specifications and estimates for submission to the Government Consulting Engineer in all instances in which the approval of the latter is required as a step precedent to the acknowledgement of claims for compensation by the Government.

Mr Haffield, Signal Dept. (£370+£25). The complete or partial destruction of 36 signal boxes has involved the necessity of prompt emergency arrangements to secure the safety of trains...

Mr Ginnetty, Running Superintendent, Loco Dept. (£575 +£50). Mr Ginnetty has had charge of the work of re-railing and clearing wrecks on numerous occasions during the past six months, and has been called upon to proceed on pilot engines through disturbed districts to ascertain whether the line was safe for traffic.

Foreman Walsh, Athlone (£350+£20). A large share of special work on the re-railing of engines and vehicles has fallen on Loco Foreman Walsh...

Wednesday 24. Baltimore Station House on the Cork Bandon & South Coast is burnt. The offices and contents, waiting room and lamproom are completely destroyed, together with part of the stationmaster's house and some of his effects. The staff instruments, telephones etc. in the office are also destroyed. The carriage shed has been demolished and the following vehicles burnt: no. 29 third class carriage; no. 19 third class carriage; no. 19 third class carriage; no. 58 first and third composite; one fish van. The estimated total damage is £4675.

Thursday 25. Part of the station premises at Blackrock on the Cork Blackrock & Passage is maliciously burnt. MGWR no. 21 *Swift* damaged at Islandeady, Co. Mayo.

Friday 26. On the GS&WR lines remaining closed include Bagnalstown to Palace East; Clara and Banaher; Kanturk and Newmarket; Thurles to Clonmel. Temporary arrangements have been entered into with Messrs. John Wallis & Son for the transfer of passenger and merchandise traffic by road between Mallow South and Mallow North stations.

On the Listowel & Ballybunion the 16.45 train from Ballybunion is held up near Francis Road station and the entire train burnt. The line is now closed as all trains have been burned, engines wrecked, and 50 per cent of the rolling stock destroyed.

Saturday 27. On the Cork Blackrock & Passage, Rochestown cabin, Monkstown station buildings and cabin, Passage Station buildings and cabin, shops, large shed, part of the coal store, blacksmith shop, six carriages, one wagon are all burnt, together with other damage.

On the D&SER the Wexford Mail, believed erroneously to be carrying Free State troops, is ambushed on the Killurin embankment by 35 to 40 Irregulars who have broken the road at Killurin station. The train, arriving as scheduled at 16.30, comes under fire killing a passenger, Lieut. Charles Burke, and injuring the fireman, William Mahony, in both legs. Finding no troops on the train the attackers restore the track and board the train which continues to Macmine Junction. There are already four trains at this station, two in the sidings, and on the through lines the 16.15 from Enniscorthy and the Waterford Mail connection are waiting in the New Ross loop. The raiders bring the Wexford Mail in on the up main line, unhook the loco, no. 67 *Rathmore*, and dispatch her towards Macmine Castle where the road has again been broken. The engine, however, stays on the rail and continues at speed through Edermine and Enniscorthy before running out of steam beyond Camolin – a run of some 29 km. Meanwhile the raiders send the Enniscorthy train out along the Wexford line to bring it back to the wrecking point. The Waterford train is also set in motion and the two collide. The raiders then run out the ballast train and the empty cattle train in the sidings which pile into the wreckage and are doused with petrol and set alight. The raiders, in three companies each with a machine gun, withdraw along the New Ross line and disperse. The ambush results in the wrecking of five trains, the complete destruction of three passenger coaches and the serious damage of four others; the complete destruction of eight merchandise vehicles and the serious damaging of six others, as well as serious damage to three engines. The cost of repair and replacement is estimated at £50,000. William Mahony, the fireman who was wounded, is to be paid full wages during his period of incapacity.

Monday 29. Four coaches are burnt at Killiney station, Co. Dublin. Repairs are urgently requested by M. F. Keogh, the D&SER General Manager, who is authorised to take on additional men at Grand Canal Street, Dublin, the railway workshops colloquially known as 'The Factory'. The GNR is to be asked to repair two engines, but there will be an eight weeks' delay.

Tuesday 30. Senator John Bagwell, General Manager of the Great Northern, is kidnapped by five armed men from his house, Drumleek, Bailey, Howth, Co. Dublin.

Wednesday 31. A breakdown train which had been engaged in removing the wreckage of a derailment near Durrow is, at about 16.20, about to return to Waterford when it is surrounded my a number of armed men. They order the GS&WR employees to leave the train and, after having been reversed through the tunnel in the direction of Durrow station to get up sufficient steam, it is sent towards the already destroyed Ballyvoile viaduct, blown up in August last year, where it fell some 9 metres. According to the *Munster Express* (3 February) 'the train hauled by 0-6-0 engine no. 189 [built in 1881] ended its journey in spectacular fashion with the engine and tender at the foot of the viaduct piers and the wagons hanging precariously over the approach embankment'. The locomotive is unrecoverable and is written off. Armed men have been visiting the homes of drivers and firemen attached to the armoured train operating in the area, enquiring of their whereabouts, and arrangements have been made for alternative accommodation.

On the D&SER the 15.15 mixed train from Macmine to Waterford is held up between Glemore and Waterford and maliciously derailed at Dog's Road Bridge (no. 457) which had been destroyed by explosives on 14 July last and replaced by a temporary structure which itself had been demolished two days later, only to be again restored. The raiders having broken the rails, the engine, 0-4-2 no. 39, with two six-wheel carriages fall down the embankment on to the County road. A wagon, the property of the GS&WR, which remains on the track is burnt. The engine and coaches are to block the County road until the end of February, when the former is retrieved and eventually restored to service. Of the coaches, nothing then remains but the wheels.

Maj. Gen. D Hogan, GOC, Dublin Command, issues a Proclamation which concludes: 'NOW WARNING is hereby given that in the event of the Senator John Bagwell not being set at liberty and permitted to return to his own home within 48 hours of the date and hour [09.00] of this Proclamation punitive action will be taken against several associates in this conspiracy, now in custody, and otherwise.'

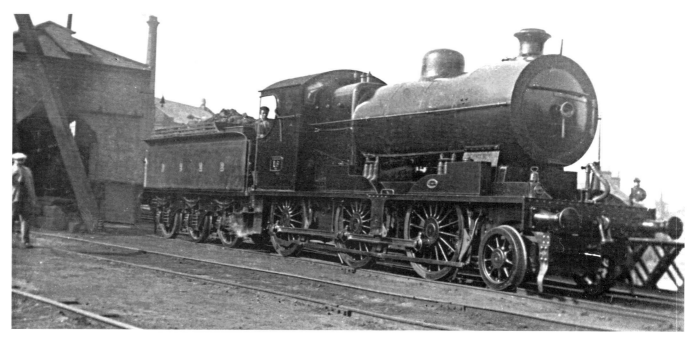

D&SER no. 16, built 1922. *See* 15 May 1922.

COAX, ORDER AND TERRORISE

Thursday 1. Tinahely signal cabin on the Shillelagh, Co Wicklow, branch of the Dublin & South Eastern is burnt. [The Dublin Wicklow & Wexford Railway opened the branch from Woodenbridge to Shillelagh on 22 May 1865. It was closed to passengers by the Great Southern on 24 April 1944 though goods trains ran from Woodenbridge as far as Aughrim until 1953].

On the West Clare a special from Ennis to Miltown Malbay is halted at Russa Bridge by ganger Mullins, about two tons of stones having been placed on the line. The obstruction removed, the train continues as far as Blackhills where several dog spikes, found driven between the joints of the rails, are removed by ganger Murphy.

In the Dáil, Domhnall Ó Ceallacháin (Wexford) asks the Minister for Industry & Commerce whether he is aware that the limited train service between Bagenalstown and Borris, which had been maintained by the Great Southern & Western Railway after the stoppage of the remainder of the branch line to Palace East by the wrecking of a train at Ballywilliam on 11 [*recte* 6] January has now been entirely suspended, whether the only reason for the suspension is that the engineer in charge of the breakdown operations at Ballywilliam sent the engines and carriages to Dublin after the breakdown train had been wrecked on another branch (Bagenalstown–Gowran) on the 14th, whether the Borris–Bagenalstown line has been profitable in working and not affected, so far, by any destructive attacks. The Minster replies to the effect that according to the company this section has been closed because 'the service it renders is not considered essential under present conditions and because it was being worked at a loss... I am considering whether I would be justified in pressing the company to re-open it'.

Senator Bagwell [see 30 January] is picked up near Swords, Co. Dublin, by a passing motorist who brings him into the city where he is afforded an interview with President Cosgrave. No statement is immediately forthcoming.

Friday 2. The GS&WR proposes to provide a temporary cattle bank at Mallow. The sum of £28,868 is due by the Government for work done for the military, and the secretary is to write to the Minister for Finance claiming payment. Counsel's opinion having been sought on the subject of malicious damage to the company's property during the British Government Control and not made good before its ending, the company is of the opinion it cannot proceed further.

(Control of the railways ended on 15 August 1921). The GS&WR's requirements for loco coal, 1500/2000 tons per week, are to be sourced from the Ebbw Vale Company of Wales at 27s 6d per ton up to the end of December. Two steam breakdown cranes are to be acquired for a total of £2000 from the Federated Engineers Ltd.

The 14.30 train ex Ennis on the West Clare is fired on from both sides of Mount Rivers bridge between Doonbeg and Shragh – about the same place as previously. Five or six shots are fired, two of which strike the engine very close to the driver and fireman's positions. On the MGWR in Co. Mayo the down train is held up and destroyed at the terminus at Killala. It is allowed to enter the station but seized after the passengers have alighted. The driver is then compelled to reverse the loco, no. 20 *Speedy,* and take the train back some distance where the carriages are fired and the engine set in forward motion. Travelling at speed it smashes through the buffers, the last on the line, and plunges into the sea. The attackers leave after setting fire to the station. [The remote 15 km extension from Ballina to Killala was opened on 2 January 1893 and closed to passengers by the Great Southern in 1931. Goods services ended three years later].

Saturday 3. On the D&SER the 23.15 suburban train from Harcourt Street to Bray is held up at Foxrock station and set on fire, two of its four coaches being destroyed. Some hundred passengers, the majority of whom are women, are told to leave the train and are compelled at gunpoint to cross the track to the up platform and enter the waiting room where they are warned to remain until further notice. When the attackers have departed after firing the train the passengers regain the down platform, the loco which has been uncoupled from the wreckage shunts two empty carriages from a siding and the reformed train continues on its journey. According to the Foxrock signalman the raiders were 'as calm and serene about the affair as any man would be during his ordinary day's work'. A male passenger said 'I was awakened by a young fellow who tapped me on the leg and said I would "have to get out" of here. When I opened my eyes I looked into the barrel of an automatic, and speedily jumped up and got out'.

The 06.00 goods and 15.00 passenger trains Limerick-Waterford on the GS&WR are wrecked between Grange station and Newcastle Junction. Both lines are blocked.

Sunday 4. Cold, wet weather. The English writer V. S. Pritchett takes a morning train from Dublin to Cork: 'A journey that normally takes two or three hours, took close on fourteen, for at Maryborough (now called Portlaoise) we stopped for the middle of the day while they got an armoured engine and troops to escort us... The afternoon faded as we went across the bogland; at Mallow it was dark, and there we got into cars to join another train across the valley. The viaduct had been blown up. We eventually arrived in Cork in a racket of machine-gun fire.'

Wednesday 7. Trains arrive in Killarney from Tralee for only the second time in six months. The first steams in at 09.30 with 30 passengers, 12 goods wagons, mail and parcels. The second arrives at 14.30 with another 30 passengers, 26 wagons, mail and parcels. Large quantities of empty bottles and containers of various kinds have accumulated in the town and carters are busy carrying them to the station.

Thursday 8. John R. Kerr, General Manager of the CB&SCR, reports that Col. Russell has called on him and informed him that the Government requires the line between Cork and Bandon to be opened at the first possible opportunity. It is agreed that a service running to and from Chetwynd viaduct is possible. Joseph Costigan, a porter at Portlaoise, is arrested at Clonkeen. He refuses to sign the usual form of undertaking and remains in gaol.

Friday 9. Tivoli station on the Cork–Youghal line of the GS&WR, which was set on fire and extensively damaged, is not to be re-opened for the present. On the same line, both names, Queenstown Junction and Cobh Junction, are to be used in future. [The Cobh Junction–Youghal section closed to all traffic in 1981 but is to be partially re-opened: the former junction station was renamed Glounthaune in 1994]. A communication from the Minister of Defence intimates that he is of the opinion that the Waterford–Wexford section should be opened as far as possible, but the GS&WR cannot at present see its way to the further opening up of this seriously damaged portion of the system. The Government Consulting Engineer has entered into an arrangement with a Mr T. Scott for the reconstruction of bridge no. 262 near Dundrum, Co. Tipperary, on the main line. The line from Tuam to Claremorris is now ready for traffic but cannot be reopened at present.

Saturday 10. Wireless message, Russell to GOC Limerick: 'What is the area like in the vicinity of Listowel–Ballybunion. With our usual methods of protection, i.e. on Nenagh Branch could we hold open. Are both bridges on road running parallel to Rly. intact. Do you consider this line important.' Reply is received on the 16th. On the Cork Blackrock & Passage the services of the stationmaster at Blackrock are to be dispensed with.

Sunday 11. An attempt is made by armed men to burn down the premises of the Cork & Muskerry at Western Road, Cork. Considerable damage is done to the station and engines.

Monday 12. The Drumshanbo agent's house on the Cavan & Leitrim is occupied by Free State troops. The station premises at Ballinglen on the Shillelagh branch of the D&SER are burnt.

Tuesday 13. The death is announced of John Fane Vernon, a Cavan man who has been chairman of the Great Northern since 1909. He was also a director of the Dundalk Newry & Greenore and a member of the Joint Committee of the City of Dublin Junction Railways, a short line built in 1891 to link Amiens Street [Connolly] and Westland Row [Pearse] across the much-maligned Liffey viaduct, popularly known as the 'Loop Line bridge'. Fane Vernon is succeeded as chairman of the GNR by the vice-chairman, William P. Cairnes.

Wednesday 14. Driver J. 'Sketch' White of the D&SER is again arrested, by three CID men accompanied by five soldiers, on the arrival of the Wexford–Dublin Mail at Bray station. Previous D&SER arrests have included fireman P. O'Sullivan at Wexford, 26 January and messenger P. Kelly at Dalkey, 12 February, who was released on Friday 16 without being charged. On the GNR Cavan branch armed men attempt the destruction of Inniskeen station.

Thursday 15. There is a further conference between management and unions at the Railway Clearing House, Dublin, to set up machinery for the negotiation of wages and conditions of service. The GS&WR is not represented and this, it is felt, may create difficulties as the unions are not disposed to enter any agreement unless it applies to all railways.

Friday 16. Wireless message GOC Limerick to Col. Russell, Wellington Barracks: 'We do not consider line Listowel to Ballybunion of importance. One post at Ballybunion would be sufficient. Our garrison at Listowel would co-operate.' Underline bridge no. 20, between Howth Junction and Portmarnock on the GNR, is destroyed.

Lady Gregory travels to Dublin to see her children off to England. 'A tiring journey...through tickets not being given – refused through – "You can't know what might happen before the end of a journey". So I had to take them at intervals, Galway to Broadstone, then to Westland Row, then to Kingstown Pier [Dun Laoghaire], then for Chicks [the children] and Eileen to Euston...'

From O/C Railway Protection, Athlone to Command Adjutant: 'Starting from tomorrow the 17th inst. patrols will leave Castlerea and Lecarrow – a section about 24 miles long. As a post has not yet been established at Lecarrow, Athlone to Lecarrow will have to be patrolled by troops from this station, if I can manage with the Local Commandant, as Lecarrow is one of the most dangerous places on this line. J. P. Adamson, Adamson Castle, Athlone.' [Lecarrow, Co Roscommon, on the Athlone-Westport line, was the site of a ballast pit, opened in 1910, supplying the railway. It was closed in 1989].

Saturday 17. Between Streamstown and Moate on the MGWR a large party of men arrive shortly after daylight and await the 07.10 Mail ex Broadstone, due to pass Mullingar at 08.25. They blow up the temporary trestle bridge that replaced the one destroyed some time ago. The Streamstown signalman is held up and the signals set against the Mail which stops at the station – passengers and company and officials are ordered out. The train is then run towards the broken bridge, resulting in serious destruction: corridor carriages and the dining car are telescoped and vans overturned. The locomotive falls over the embankment into a field. The driver, interviewed after the event, says that when the train was brought to a standstill three or four men carrying rifles approached the engine and ordered him and the fireman to step down, leaving them on the platform with the passengers. One of the men got onto the loco and set it in motion, sending the train heading down the gradient into the wrecked bridge. The following Mullingar–Claremorris special of empty wagons is also stopped and run into the wreck but little damage ensues. The men also stop a heavy up goods from Ballina on the Moate side of the Streamstown bridge. When it comes to a halt they uncouple the engine and send it at high speed into the wreckage. 'Three trains piled up in a heap as high as a big house', says an observer at the scene. The Mail passengers are stranded in Streamstown until 14.30 by which time a new temporary bridge has been erected. Traffic is being maintained by routing trains from Athlone via the GS&WR to Clara and thence via Horseleap to Streamstown, with similar working in the down direction. [The short 13 km MGWR link between Streamstown and Clara dated from 1863, the latter small town in its railway heyday boasting two stations. Interrupted, as were so many small branch line services during the Emergency [aka World War II] by shortage of fuel, it closed both for passengers and regular goods in 1947, though it saw occasional specials until 1949 and was subsequently used for wagon storage until 1963. The link closed completely in 1965 and was lifted the following year].

Monday 19. On the CB&SCR, 21 men are now employed running trains to Bandon, utilising two engines with two on protection duty. From Saturday last works trains have been running across the viaduct and a passenger service between Cork and Bandon will operate from tomorrow. Passengers, however, will have temporarily to change trains at the viaduct while staging is being got ready for the putting in place of the fourth rib, though it is hoped before next week to be able to run trains through from Cork to Bandon and back for goods and livestock as well as passengers.

The two new locos on the West Clare, 4-6-0T nos. 3, *Ennistymon* and 7, *Malbay*, have successfully completed their 1000 miles trial.

Tuesday 20. An engine and two wagons have been armoured at the GNR Dundalk works by order of the Free State military authorities. Applications are to be made to the Government for payment £760, the cost of the work.

The MGWR awards Special Grants for Meritorious Services. Driver J. Geraghty, Athlone: derailment of three engines on Achill Branch, 10 January 1923 (£10); Driver P. Cassidy: holdup of a special of stock, Kilfree, 20 January 1923. (£5); Driver R. Cole and Fireman M. Egan, Mullingar: holdup of 08.45 ex Sligo, 30 January 1923 (£5 each); Loco Foremen McKay, Mullingar and Rorison, Sligo: derailment of rolling stock at Streamstown and Sligo [*dates not given*] (£10 each).

William Crolly, the GS&WR engine driver wounded when his train was fired on at Castleconnell on the 12th last, dies from his wounds in Dr Steevens's Hospital, Dublin. He was the first GS&WR driver to refuse to carry Black & Tans and was threatened with death on three occasions.

On the Cork City tramway system a bomb is discovered pressed down between the points in one of the tracks at the Electric Power House. One tramcar has passed over it without setting off an explosion, but all returning trams are held up until the missile has been removed.

Thursday 22. On the Cork & Muskerry, steamraiser Connell and fireman Buckley of Coachford have been arrested by the military and are still in custody. A letter from Miss Maud Walsh to the Dublin United Tramway Co. expresses her appreciation of the conduct of motorman John Quinn and conductor W. Hand during firing at College Green yesterday.

At the inquest on William Crolly, Barrack Street, Nenagh (see 20th above) ticket collector John Mulligan states than on the 13th of this month he saw the deceased in St John's Hospital, Limerick. He told him that when driving the 6 pm train with passengers and goods from Limerick to Nenagh and when about 2 ½ miles from Castleconnell he heard what he believed to be fog signals and slowed down the train. He then saw a red light in front of him on the line and on approaching it felt a stinging pain in his left elbow and another in his left hip. He knew then that the train had been ambushed. The train was afterwards set on fire. He saw a number of men about the train and one said he was sorry he had been injured. The finding of the inquest is that death was due to blood poisoning from infected gunshot wounds.

Friday 23. The 13.00 D&SER train ex Waterford is boarded by armed men who have previously tampered with the rails at bridge no. 367 south of the station. They order the driver off the footplate and set the train in motion towards the bridge, where the tender of the engine is derailed and as a consequence the chairs of the permanent way are broken.

The Minister for Industry & Commerce is enquiring as to when the line between Waterford and Durrow can be opened. He is informed that the GS&WR do not propose to open it until the bridge is renewed. A contract for Enginemen's pilot pea jackets is to be given to the Inchicore Sewing Class. [A pea jacket is a short, heavy overcoat of coarse cloth].

Killarney remains isolated as a result of the destruction of the bridge at Ardagh and no trains, food supplies or other goods have reached the town since the 14th. The linesmen were notified some days ago that their services were dispensed with: yesterday, however, the were told to resume work, suggesting that a service might be about to resume. In the meantime intending travellers are obliged to walk or drive the 34 km to Tralee to access trains on the North Kerry line to Limerick and beyond.

Saturday 24. A letter is received by the D&SER Waterford agent: 'Headquarters, Waterford Brigade, IRA, 23/2/23. Warning is hereby given that unless a guarantee is given in the Public press within 48 hours of receipt of this Order that the following are not conveyed by train the Crews of the Railway Engines will be fired on by our Troops without further notice. 1. Enemy Troops whether armed or unarmed. 2. Enemy Intelligence officers. 3. Supplies of all kinds intended for Enemy Troops. 4. Communications of Enemy. Signed Brigade O/C.' It is decided that similar letters received by the agents should be published in the press as an item of news.

Monday 26. An Organisation memorandum prepared for the General H/Q Staff by the Railway Protection Corps gives its present strength as 3022. It lists the methods employed by the Irregulars in the destruction of railways:
(1) Destruction of Bridges, Viaducts, Culverts, Cattle passes 'A' by Explosions; 'B' by Acetyline Gas Welding Burners; 'C' without either 'A' or 'B' by hand tools, crow-bars against masonry work, etc.
(2) Destruction of Chairs and Fish-Plates, i.e. the fittings for securing the rails to the sleepers without removing rails – which result in derailments due to spreading of rails.
(3) Removal of rails by knocking out wooden Keys and Bolts from Fish-Plates (i.e. regular method of removing a rail).
(4) Placing of stone and sleeper barricades across rails.
(5) Flagging and holding up of trains. Detaching engine and running it into carriages. Burning of carriages. Raiding trains for mail and goods.
(6) Burning of Signal Cabins, Stations etc.
(7) Sniping of trains.

(8) Raiding of Loco. Depots for Engines in steam, and causing damage such as recently happened at Kildare, Inchicore, Sligo.

The Memorandum details the present tactics for the prevention of destruction as
(1) Establishment of Blockhouses on important Bridges, Tunnels and Viaducts.
(2) Establishment of Blockhouses between Sections for the purpose of preventing holds-up, such as described.
(3) Establishment of Posts on Stations, Signal Cabins, Loco. Depots.
(4) Lancia car and Armoured Train Patrols.
(5) Guarding of Passenger Trains – by moving troops on the train from one post to another.
(6) Establishment of Railway Police Section on Loco. Depots at Cork.
(7) Intelligence.
(8) Infantry Co-operation.

Among the difficulties encountered it cites the fact that the railway companies are putting all the repair work on the Corps, the lack of funds and the 'anti-Government attitude of a number of highly-placed Officials and Railway Workmen (especially GS&WR); A collection of Anti-Free State and Anti-Republican highly-placed officials, combined with a sprinkling of English die-hard Unionist shareholders'. With specific regard to the GS&WR 'it is now necessary, in connection with this Company, to coax, order and terrorise, alternately, in order that the temporary repairs may be carried out. Internal difficulties include those of securing supplies from the Quartermaster Generals' Department to meet current demands for clothing, equipment, stationery stores and road transport, difficulties which have considerably retarded the development of the 'General Scheme'. In fact, the Memorandum concludes, 'at the moment the Corps progress is at a complete standstill'. Óglaigh na hÉireann [the Free State Army] nevertheless advertises for recruits for the Corps.

The Rt. Hon. Sir Stanley Harrington, Chairman of the Cork Blackrock & Passage, tells shareholders present at the Annual General Meeting in Cork that the past year has been the most disastrous ever experienced by several of the Irish railways. 'In common with many others in Southern Ireland we have suffered heavily. To begin with, a strike lasting nearly a month took place in February 1922, inflicting serious loss on the Company and grave inconvenience to the travelling public and the commercial community; but this was nothing to what happened later on in the year. On August 8 one of the spans of the Douglas viaduct was maliciously destroyed by explosives and in consequence it has not been possible ever since to run any trains whatsoever...Furthermore, at the end of January last the station buildings and signal cabins at Blackrock, Monkstown and Passage were burned to the ground by raiders, also the signal cabin at Rochestown, and in addition at Passage the workshops were seriously damaged and several carriages burned to cinders...' The paddle-steamers *Hibernia* and *Albert* are providing alternative passenger services, together with two goods steamers, the public having been left only three days without connections with Cork and other stations.'

Wednesday 28. At the Annual General Meeting of the Great Southern & Western Railway Co., held at Kingsbridge Terminus, Dublin, the Chairman, William J. Goulding, informs the shareholders that 'during the year your property has been subject to an intense campaign of destruction by the Forces opposed to the Government of the Free State. From the very commencement of hostilities your Railway has been a principal object of attack, being apparently looked upon as the lines of communication of the National Army, and therefore damaged with the object of preventing the movement of the National Troops...Towards the end of the year the financial position of your Company, owing to the above effects of the Civil War which suspended our receipts, coupled with the high rates of wages, was such that we would probably be unable to meet expenses, and the Board submitted for the consideration of the Government that they should come to our assistance in the crisis on the ground that the railways have been damaged and bridges and works destroyed because (a) they are regarded as being the lines of communication of the National Army, and (b) it is desired by the destruction of communication to make government impossible.

We pointed out that the maintenance of lines of communication should be regarded as part of the necessary cost of the war, and should be borne by the Nation, instead of throwing the obligation on the Shareholders, and asked for terms similar to those granted by the British Government during the European War. The Government declined to do this or even to meet the payment of Debenture Interest...Under these circumstances your Directors considered it advisable in the interests of the Proprietors to continue the running of the Railway as long as possible in their own hands'. Shareholders are furnished with a map showing malicious damage to the Company's property from 28 June to 31 December 1922, both days inclusive. It shows 375 instances of permanent way damage; 207 underbridges damaged; 48 overbridges; 71 signal cabins completely destroyed and 12 damaged; 13 buildings destroyed by fire and 47 engines, carriages and other rolling stock derailed or destroyed. There were 200 cases of stations and trains raided and goods stolen'.

38 shopmen and 24 running men have been employed on the CB&SCR during the past week. All the rolling stock between Cork and Bandon has been examined, overhauled and oiled, and is now ready for traffic. The line has opened between Cork, Clonakilty and Ballineen, with full pay restored on the open sections.

Joseph McGrath, Minister for Industry & Commerce, asks for a meeting on 1 March of himself and Government representatives with the Chairman and General Manager of the Dublin & South Eastern in connection with the re-opening of lines now closed. Mr Neale, General Manager and Mr Wordley will meet him. The Minister also suggests that troops used for protection purposes should be conveyed over the railways free of charge. A decision on this is postponed by the D&SER board.

Today the *Irish Independent* prints a lengthy and enthusiastic report on the role of Railway Repair & Maintenance Corps. 'It is frequently the case that a nation knows little or nothing about some of its best servants', it suggests: 'the average Irishman knows that it [the Corps] exists, and that occasionally some of its members are killed in the execution of their duty and there his knowledge ends'. One of the principal factors that contribute to the success of the Corps, the paper suggests, is its personnel. 'It is not easy to find men who can do highly technical work and fight gallantly against heavy odds as well, but Colonel Russell found them. He recruited the rank and file mainly from unemployed railwaymen and his officers from the National Army, Government Departments especially the Ordnance Survey Department and Ministry of Labour, and from railway officials.' The Corps, it is explained, is divided into eight Commands corresponding to the Army Commands, in charge of a Commandant who is a qualified engineer. 'At his HQ he has an armoured train always ready to rush to any part of the line at a moment's notice...If the work to be done is sufficiently extensive to keep them engaged overnight a couple of wagons to be used as sleeping quarters are hitched on. These armoured trains carry out all extreme repairs'. 'The Command', the report continues, 'is subdivided into companies and the companies into groups of "posts". These latter carry out patrol work and minor repairs. The "post" is usually a blockhouse built of railway sleepers, sandbags and corrugated iron and contains about 20 men under a sergeant...the captain generally lives at the nearest railway station where he has his company HQ.' Of the morale of the Corps, 'their Colonel, who is in a position to know, can proudly boast that his men have cheerfully endured hardships that even the troops in Flanders, under the iron discipline of the British Army, would have mutinied rather than submit to. "They will stand anything", he declares, "because they know that as soon as it is humanly possible the conditions will be improved and because meanwhile their officers share their discomforts." Life in a blockhouse is every bit as uncomfortable as life in a dugout, and persistent sniping at it at night heightens the resemblance'.

Thursday 1. The Cork Blackrock & Passage receives a letter from R. Crawford, Secretary, GS&WR on the subject of the proposed grouping scheme: he is seeking financial information. D&SER porters Michael Dowling and Patrick Conroy, Dalkey, are arrested by the military and lodged in Mountjoy Jail. On 20 April the Minister for Defence will announce their imminent release.

March

márta

1923

Friday 2. Dublin County Council have received a claim from the D&SER for £10,325 in respect of the burning of trains and damage to the permanent way, and from the GNR for £3000 for damage to the bridge between Malahide and Portmarnock, blown up on 16 February last.

Saturday 3. Athy, Co Kildare, station and goods store are burned.

Sunday 4. Special trains bring Munster supporters to Dublin to the postponed 1921 All-Ireland Hurling Final at Croke Park, Limerick defeating Dublin 8–5 to 4–2 and becoming the first holders of the MacCarthy Cup.

Monday 5. A Dublin & South Eastern carriage shop cleaner, P. O'Higgins, is arrested by the military. The 15.15 train ex Macmine Junction, carrying military and civilians, is fired upon by Irregular forces about 2 km from Glemore station on the D&SER. Carriages occupied by troops are riddled with bullets, seven windows are broken in carriage no. 112, and one civilian is reported injured. The train stops and the troops detrain and return fire. The attackers flee and are pursued into the surrounding hills but make good their escape.

The Dublin–Limerick goods, GS&WR, is wrecked at Trumera between Portlaoise and Mountrath by a break in the line. This results in the derailment of 26 wagons, it is believed by the placing of a mine underneath them. The whole centre of the train is a complete wreck: furniture, artificial manure, meal, chests of tea and boxes of merchandise of all kinds lie exposed. The goods are being guarded by troops and men of the Railway Corps and a repair gang from Inchicore is clearing the line. Passengers using the main line are for the present obliged to leave trains at the blockage and make their way along a high narrow bank to continue their journey.

Tuesday 6. The mixed 17.00 Tralee–Limerick, with livestock and perishables, is held up at Barnagh station when it arrives there at 19.00. The passengers are ordered out and the train set on fire and sent at high speed down the gradient towards Newcastle West which is a terminal station, involving arriving trains having to reverse out to continue the journey to Limerick. The blazing train, which can be seen from a considerable distance, runs into the buffer stop at the station and the locomotive, together with four carriages, two covered vans and six open wagons, topples into a field near a timber yard, burning furiously. The last three wagons are saved, including one containing pigs, 23 out of 25 of which are liberated alive. The passengers removed at Barnagh have to walk the 10 km along the track to Newcastle West. [The line from Newcastle West to Tralee was opened by the Limerick & Kerry Railway on 20 December 1880, completing the North Kerry line from Limerick. The entire line was closed to passengers by CIÉ on 4 February 1963, but goods services ran from Listowel to Tralee until 1977].

Wednesday 7. D&SER fireman J. Hammond, Bray, is arrested by the military. In the Dáil, William Davin (Laois-Offaly) asks the Minister for Industry & Commerce if he is aware that the GS&WR's quarry at Lisduff station has been closed since June 1922 with the result that nearly 150 men are out of employment since that period. The Minister responds that he has had representations made to the company, 'but it states that it does not require to distribute ballast in its northern area and cannot economically supply ballast from Lisduff for use in its southern area. Moreover, as the quarry is in an isolated district the company fears that the plant and hopper wagons would be damaged if working was resumed'.

Thursday 8. Work is partly resumed in the Rocksavage, Cork fitting shop of the CB&SCR on locomotives nos. 2, 10 and 16. The 11.55 Goods from Maryborough [Portlaoise] is derailed at milepost 4½ between Conniberry Junction and Abbeyleix on the Portlaoise–Kilkenny line of the GS&WR. The loco, 0-6-0 no. 174, built in 1889, is derailed but recovered, to remain in service until 1953. [The line from Portlaoise to Kilkenny via Abbeyleix opened from Abbelyleix to Kilkenny in 1865 and from Portlaoise to Abbeyleix two years later. It was closed in its entirety in 1963, ending the alternative through route from Dublin to Waterford].

Friday 9. Free conveyance of troops is approved by the GS&WR [see 28 February].

Saturday 10. Grange Con station, on the Sallins–Tullow, Co. Wicklow branch on the GS&WR, is burned down. A goods special is derailed between Grange and Waterford.

Tuesday 13. Rathvilly station, Co. Carlow, also on the Sallins-Tullow line, is burned.

Wednesday 14. In a further attack on the Tullow line Colbinstown station is burned. It is reported that preliminary agreements having an important bearing on the grouping of the railways have

49
W. H. Moxton, locomotive superintendent,
Midland Great Western, 1915–25.

50
Officers and men of the Engineering Division, Cork
Command, Railway Corps.

51
J.R. Bazin, Chief Mechanical
Engineer, GS&WR.
See 15 May 1922.

52
J.B Wilson. General Manager,
Cork & Muskerry.

53
Lady Gregory at Coole.
See 16 April 1922.

54
The Cork, Bandon & South Coast
at Bantry, Co. Cork.
See 20 August 1922.

55
Castle Junction, Belfast.
See 12 February 1922.

56
MGWR train approaching
Mallaranny (Mulrany) Co. Mayo.
See 3 May 1922.

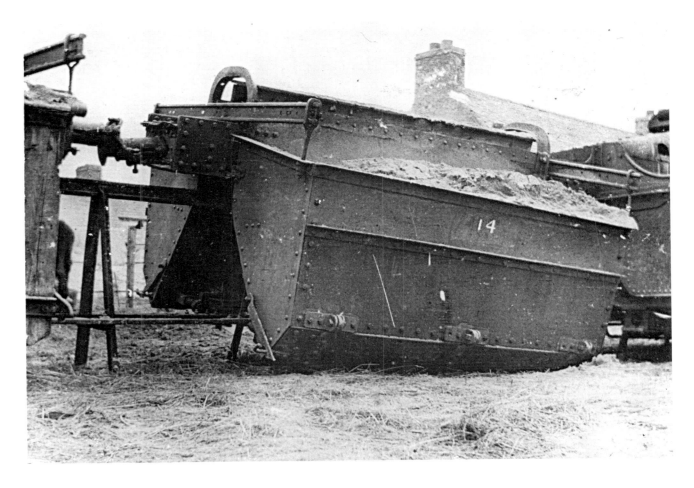

57
Derailment on
the Listowel &
Ballybunnion
See 17 January
1923.

58
Loco no. 6 under
examination on
the West Clare.
See 21 April 1922.

59
Trams in Cork.
See 24 August 1922.

60
Attack on the Cork & Muskerry,
date unknown.

61
Activity at Achill Sound station,
Co. Mayo.
See 10 January 1923.

62
Kilmessan junction.
See 23 January 1923.

63
Branch line
scene, Oldcastle
Co. Meath, on
the Great
Northern.

64
Passage station,
Cork, Blackrock
and Passage.
See 25 August
1922.

65

D&SER no. 17 *Wicklow* wrecked on Ballyanne bank, Rathgarogue, Co. Wexford on 27 January 1923. This ill-fated locomotive had been involved in the accident at Harcourt Street terminus, Dublin on 14 February 1900 when it failed to stop and crashed through the end wall of the station.

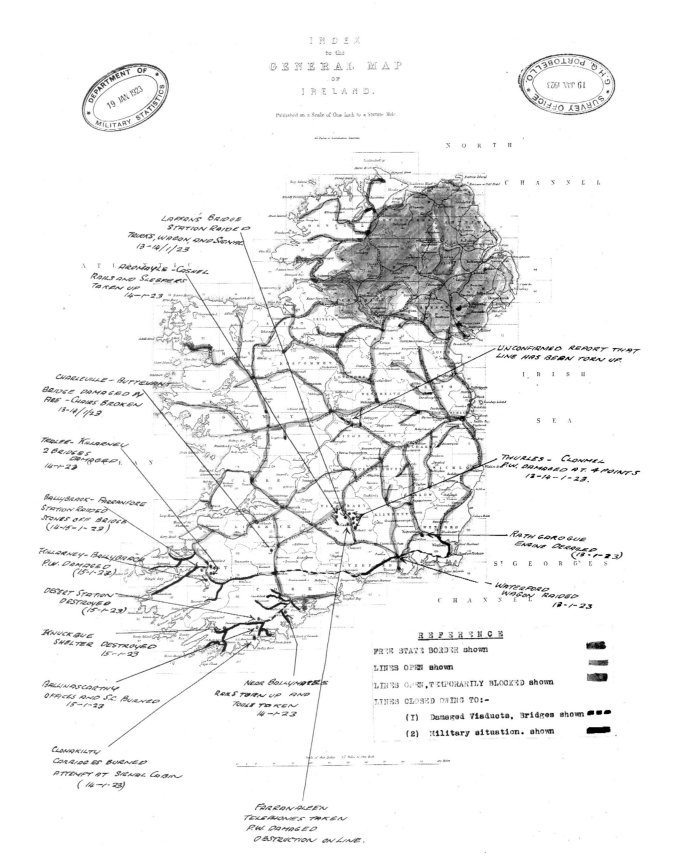

INDEX
to the
GENERAL MAP
OF
IRELAND.

Published on a Scale of One Inch to a Statute Mile.

LAFFAN'S BRIDGE
STATION RAIDED
TRUCKS, WAGON, AND SIGNAL
13-14/1/23

LAROMAYLE - CASHEL
RAILS AND SLEEPERS
TAKEN UP
14-1-23

CHARLEVILLE - BUTTEVANT
BRIDGE DAMAGED BY
FIRE - CHAIRS BROKEN
13-14/1/23

TRALEE - KILLARNEY
2 BRIDGES
DAMAGED
14-1-23

BALLYBRACK - FARRANFORE
STATION RAIDED
STONES OFF BRIDGE
(14-15-1-23)

KILLARNEY - BALLYBRACK
P.W. DAMAGED
(15-1-23)

DESERT STATION
DESTROYED
(15-1-23)

KNUCKBUE
SHELTER DESTROYED
15-1-23

BALLINASCARTHY
OFFICES AND S.C. BURNED
15-1-23

CLONAKILTY
CARRIDGES BURNED
ATTEMPT AT SIGNAL CABIN
(14-1-23)

NEAR BALLYMAREE
RAILS TORN UP AND
TOOLS TAKEN
14-1-23

FARRANALEEN
TELEPHONES TAKEN
P.W. DAMAGED
OBSTRUCTION ON LINE.

UNCONFIRMED REPORT THAT
LINE HAS BEEN TORN UP.

THURLES - CLONMEL
P.W. DAMAGED AT. 4 POINTS
13-14-1-23.

RATH GAROGUE
ENGINE DERAILED
(13-1-23)

WATERFORD
WAGON RAIDED
13-1-23

IN TIME OF CIVIL WAR

been entered into on behalf of the principal companies, though the managers are reticent in discussing the subject.

Communique from Army HQ: 'A party of Irregulars seized a railway engine yesterday morning at Monksland between Thomastown and Athlone. An officer of the Railway Protection Corps, who saw the engine pass through Athlone station, communicated with the first blockhouse on the line along which the engine travelled. This was situated at 73 milepost. Volunteer Brady, who was on duty at the post, divested himself of his boots and socks and awaited the oncoming engine. As the train passed at a speed of 20 to 30 miles per hour Volunteer Brady pluckily jumped onto the footplate and succeeded in reaching the controls and bringing the engine to a standstill about 500 yards from an oncoming passenger train. Volunteer Brady was injured about the feet, but not seriously.' [The Mullingar–Moate–Athlone line, formerly part of the MGWR main line from Dublin to Galway, was opened in 1851. It was closed to all traffic except engineers' trains in 1987 but remains in situ. It featured prominently, if anonymously, in the 1978 film *The First Great Train Robbery*].

Thursday 15. On the MGWR Ballina branch near Foxford a rail is lifted at a bridge spanning a river. A serious catastrophe is averted by a farmer's daughter who waves a green flag and brings the morning Mail to a standstill within a metre of the breakage. The body of Nicholas Corcoran, an Irregular leader killed yesterday, is on the train, being conveyed to his native place in Galway and the passengers include 14 soldiers and five wounded men.

Military guards, if required, are to be given free travelling facilities on the West Clare in common with the practice of the larger companies.

Friday 16. At midnight there is an armed raid on the Dublin United Tramways Co.'s Cabra depot, dating from the horse tram era of the 1870s. The raiders leave with the sum of £46. 13s. 5d. E. A. Neale, General Manager, GS&WR, reports the result of the interview which he and his colleague Mr Woodley had on Tuesday last with Professor Whelehan and Messrs Campbell and Ingram of the Ministry of Industry & Commerce respecting the lines on which no trains are presently running. It was agreed that a train service may be run on trial and further reported on. Consideration is given to the company's liability under the Workmen's Compensation Act where its servants are injured in ambushes, the wrecking of trains etc. Further cases have arisen and the board decides that ordinary compensation be paid. Its attention is drawn to a statement made by the President in the Dáil on 23 February regarding the repair of Fota Bridge, Cobh [Belvelly viaduct] which, it is suggested, is at variance with the facts.

Monday 19. Palace East station on the D&SER suffers attack.

Tuesday 20. Joseph Hunt and John Brien, both of Little Bray, Co. Wicklow, are arrested by the military who find them tampering with the slot locks in the gentleman's lavatory in Bray station. Sir George S. Clark, Bart. is appointed Deputy Chairman of the GNR. Authority is given for £50 to be lent to Mr F. J. O'Reilly, stationmaster, Ballyward, who was shot on 23 September 1922 and is not yet fit to resume duty. [The station, on the GNR line from Knockmore Junction to Castlewellan, Co. Down, was opened in 1906. The line was closed completely in 1955]. The GNR board receives details of the proposed arrangements for Customs examination at stations adjoining the boundary between the Irish Free State and Northern Ireland, and authority is given for the hutments asked for at the frontier posts to be provided. The separation of the fiscal systems of the Irish Free State and the UK is to take place on the night of 31 March/1 April, introducing customs and excise barriers, which will seriously affect the cross-border railways.

Wednesday 21. The 18.50 Ballingrane–Foynes is completely burned at Foynes. [This branch off the Limerick–Tralee line was opened to Foynes in 1858 and closed to passengers in 1963. Though still in situ with the potential of serving an expanding port, it is now reduced (2006) to the status of an 'engineer's siding', with no traffic].

Thursday 22. John R. Kerr, CB&SCR General Manager, reports that he has visited Dublin and ascertained that the grouping scheme has more or less come to a standstill owing to the differences of opinion between the railway companies and to the political difficulty of dealing with the Great Northern company.

Friday 23. Inch station on the D&SER is burnt. In the Dáil, the President, W. T. Cosgrave, informs the House that repairs to the Mallow viaduct have proceeded as far as possible, pending accurate measurements being obtained. The GS&WR was unable to produce these and they cannot be obtained until the debris of the fallen bridge is removed. This latter work was delayed, he says, by the dock strike in Cork and the flooding of the River Blackwater, but it is now being progressed. 'There has been a considerable difficulty', he adds, 'in coming to an understanding with the railway company in regard to the repair of these large bridges, but such difficulties are not now expected to cause delay.'

Saturday 24. From HQ, 4th Infantry Batt., Claremorris Command, Renmore Barracks, Galway [Free State Army]: 'An attempt was made to blow up Lough Gannon bridge, 1½ miles west of Ross Railway Station between Ross and Oughterard. The attempt was partly successful. The bridge was not blown up but a rail was displaced. At the same time a party of armed men boarded the train at Ross station and compelled the engine driver to drive towards Lough Gannon bridge which was supposed to have been blown up. The brake van and another carriage were derailed. The damage was only slight, and the trains were running again the same evening. A report of the above having been received I detailed Capt. Dundon with a party of men to proceed to Lough Gannon bridge, where he was joined by a cycle patrol under Capt. O'Dea, but on their arrival the armed men had decamped.' [*signed*] Comndt.

Monday 26. Kilmessan station on the MGWR is again burned and all books and documents are destroyed. [Kilmessan, the junction off the Navan line for Athboy via Trim, was opened in 1864 and closed to passengers in 1947. A weekly livestock train ran until 1953].

Contrary to the report of the 14th last, it is stated 'on excellent authority' that the railway companies have failed to frame the schemes of grouping which, under the railway Agreement, they are required to submit to the Government by this Saturday. A proposed arrangement for the union of the GNR and MGWR is said to be 'dead off'.

Tuesday 27. At the request of the military an armoured train is being fitted at the D&SER Factory [Grand Canal Street Works, Dublin].

Thursday 29. The GS&WR 16.30 Waterford–Limerick is fired on near Kilsheelan station. Two passengers are wounded.

April
aibreán
1923

Easter Sunday 1. An armed raid at the Sandymount office of the Dublin United Tramway Co. results in the robbing of £14. 4. 0. The Traffic Manager, D. Brophy, explains to the directors that all possible precautions in this matter were being operated.

Wednesday 4. The last train from Cork on the Cork & Macroom is held up at Firmount and five soldiers are taken out and searched by armed men.

Thursday 5. The Railway Protection Corps is now establishing posts along the Bantry Bay Extension Railway and the debris of Scart Road bridge is to be removed from the line which is expected to re-open next week. [The Bantry Bay Extension Railway, from Bantry town to Bantry pier, was opened to passengers in 1909 by the CB&SCR which had absorbed the former company. It closed to passengers in 1937 and completely in 1949].

At a meeting of the Dublin Port & Docks Board a letter is read from the Dublin Chamber of Commerce enquiring if the Board has any information as to the terms of railway grouping which would preserve the normal geographical routes and prevent the diversion of traffic from Dublin port and cattle market. The chairman, Senator Moran, says that when they wrote to the Minister of Transport in connection with the matter and asked him to receive a deputation, he pointed out that officially he had heard nothing in connection with the proposed grouping. Anything he had seen in the newspapers was to the effect that the railway companies had failed to come to an agreement, and it was left to the Government to step in.

Friday 6. The GS&WR receives a paying order for £2500 from the Disposal & Liquidation Commission, London, in full discharge of all claims for rent and reinstatement in respect of the occupation by the British Government of the land at Waterford on which they erected a shell factory. The General Manager, E. A. Neale, seeks authority to purchase 12 hogsheads of Jameson's whiskey at 5s 6d per proof gallon net, also six hogsheads of port wine at £31.10.0 per pipe, less 5 percent, for the Hotels Dept. Meanwhile S. J. Medcalf, Hotels Manager, is kept prisoner by Irregular forces for four and a half hours on the Kerry hills. They steal his kit bag and personal effects to the value of about £15. 2s. 8d. The Irregular activist Jeremiah Murphy recalled: 'about a dozen of us were standing on the road at Poulgorm Bridge when a touring car came along from the direction of Ballyvourney. The occupants, besides the driver, were a man and a woman intending to open the great Southern Hotels in Kenmare and Parknasilla. It also contained several cases of liquor. Our officers decided to use the car to drive us to the bridge at Killaha [over the Flesk, recently re-opened by Government forces] and destroy it'. Goods in transit to the Kenmare Hotel are taken to the value of £8. 10s. 9d.

The bridge at Grange on the Dundalk Newry & Greenore between Greenore and Bush stations is destroyed. Troops from Greenore and Dundalk scour the district as far as Carlingford.

Saturday 7. The house of Mrs Tynan, Errill, Lisduff, is raided by armed men on account of her son serving in the Railway Protection Corps at Thurles. They search the premises, leaving with the sum of £14. 9s. 0d.

Sunday 8. A motorcyclist and a companion in a sidecar figure in an attack on the outpost manned by Free State troops at Clontarf station, Dublin. At about 20.35 the cyclist drives the machine up to the wicket gate giving access to the platform and before he can be challenged the man in the sidecar rises to his feet and hurls three bombs through the window of the waiting-room. They explode, shattering the windows and causing much damage to the furniture and fittings. Pte. J. Cassidy, who is sitting in the room, is struck by bomb splinters in the forehead and knocked unconscious. Simultaneously with the throwing of the bombs heavy revolver fire is opened on the troops by snipers located in thickets near the station, under cover of which the motorcyclist and his passenger make good their escape.

Traffic on the GNR main line is blocked by mine expolsions at Fane bridge at the Commons, Drumiskin and the Haynestown metal bridge 1 km nearer Dundalk.

Monday 9. The temporary bridge at the Douglas viaduct on the Cork Blackrock & Passage is nearing completion. Athboy station, terminus of the 20 km MGWR branch from Kilmessan Junction, Co. Meath, is completely wrecked. The military guard was withdrawn a week ago. {Kilmessan–Athboy was opened on 26 February 1864 by the Dublin & Meath Railway. It closed to passengers on 27 January 1947 and completely on 15 January 1954].

Tuesday 10. Drogheda Command of the Railway Protection Corps Daily Summary No. 1: 'On the 7th at 3.30 pm 5382 Vol. Tierney when returning from village of Dromin to his post at the station, with purchases for his comrades, was held up by armed men in a motor car, who took him off the main road and had a consultation as to whether they would shoot him or otherwise. Eventually they brought him some distance in the car and stripped him of his uniform, cap, boots and leggings and also took his paybook. They asked him questions concerning the strength of posts which he answered giving false information. He was allowed to go and returned to his post.' Thurles Command reports information has been received to the effect that Eamon de Valera is operating with a large Irregular column in the vicinity of Dundrum, Co Tipperary.

At 05.45 the MGWR North Wall-Kingscourt goods is held up at Batterstown, Co. Meath. The driver and fireman are ordered off and two men mount the footplate and drive the train to Drumree, the next station, where they attempt to open a petrol tank wagon. Failing in this, they then send the train ahead at speed to Knockmark, some 3 km distant, where a rail has been lifted. The engine jumps the rails, falling into the ditch, and several wagons are smashed. The single line is completely blocked.

Wednesday 11. Fethard station, on the line from Thurles to Clonmel, is heavily attacked from 20.00 to 23.30. A detachment of the Railway Protection Corps replies with rifles and Lewis guns. At 23.23 the Irregulars congregate in force near the bridge and put in a heavy fire on the station. O/C Detachment fires a rifle grenade and screams and groans are heard when it bursts. Firing ceases.

Thursday 12. At night, Chapel station, on the D&SER line between Macmine Junction and Palace East, is burned down by armed men, who also burn the stationmaster's house. A permanent way travelling hut is being erected at the station for the temporary use of the stationmaster and his family.

Friday 13. All Drogheda Command posts of the Railway Protection Corps are on alert owing to rumours of concentration of Irregulars in the area between Drogheda and the border. Escorts are sent on all trains travelling after 19.00 between Drogheda and Dundalk. Eight boxes of 'Ideal Salt' consigned to Ballymote, Co. Sligo, from Belfast are examined at Streamstown and found to contain high explosive.

Sunday 15. A consignment from Belfast to Palace East on the D&SER is also described as 'eight cases of Ideal Salt'. They are consigned to one Doyle, together with a bag addressed to Miss Kathleen Lyne of Palace House, which was a clandestine Irregular centre of operations until occupied by Free State forces in February 1923. The consignment lies unclaimed in the station siding for a week until the garrison in Palace House run out of salt and seek to replenish their supply. On being opened the cases are found to contain high explosives which are taken over by the military and signed for by Lieut. Leary.

Instructions are issued by Dublin Command of the Railway Protection Corps for a search to be made of Rectory Lodge, Raheny. The following is reported by the O i/c: 'On evening of 15th, proceeded to Raheny and surrounded the Lodge. Occupants were absent. We gained admittance and made thorough search. A letter from a prisoner in Newbridge Barracks was found, and the principal correspondents of the tenants appear to be M. McKenna, 20 Burlington Road, Dublin; Mrs Sutton, Riverside Cottage, Kinsealy, and a person (unnamed) of 1, Bulk Lane, Clonmel. Mrs Drury, wife of the Rector, stated the occupant of the Lodge, Jas. Mullen, was out of her employment, but refused to give up tenancy – also the Lodge is full of people at night, and men leave there at 4 am. A girl name Lizzie Rice, of 2nd House, Strand Road, Raheny, employed at the Rectory as a casual worker, is also under suspicion. A path which runs through the Rectory grounds to Railway Embankment at Down Distant Signal could be used at night to reach the Railway Line.'

Monday 16. Claremorris Command of the Railway Protection Corps reports that 'McNally's house at the 148 mile post (near Castlebar) is being used as a resting place by three Irregulars, Gavin, Duffy and Gibbons. On 13th fifteen armed men visited four houses on the Westport–Castlebar road, warning men to leave the country within 24 hours. The Irregular leader, Moane, was seen in the vicinity of Islandeady on the same date. Women known to be carrying dispatches for Irregulars in Westport – a woman searcher badly needed in that area'. Clonmel Command reports that Irregulars called at Landscape, the residence of Mrs Kingston, and demanded Dog Licences [see Monday 23 below]. When these were refused they stole a bicycle.

Tuesday 17. Claremorris Command, RPR&MC, advises that on the night of 15/16 an attack was made on the residence of Lord Oranmore. The building, which is situated 2.5 km from Claremorris, is being taken over by GOC Claremorris as Command HQ. Drogheda supplies information concerning a dump in a graveyard at Dromin, about 2.5 km from the Post. On a search being carried out, the tunic, breeches, leggings, cap and pay book taken from Vol. Tierney were discovered, as well as two clips of .303 ammunition and the remains of corned beef and biscuits.

In the Dáil, Thomas Johnson (Co. Dublin) asks the Minister for Industry & Commerce – on behalf of fellow-TD W. Davin – if he is aware that the Cork & Macroom railway has been completely closed down for the past eight months and whether it is a fact that no attempt has been made to re-open the line for traffic although the damage to be repaired is comparatively trivial; and if he will consider the desirability of bringing pressure to bear upon the company to makethe necessary arrangements for re-opening without further delay. Patrick Hogan, Minister for Agriculture, replying for his colleague, tells the Deputy that 'proposals have been received from the company for the principal repairs necessary on this railway, and have been approved. The difficulty has not been so much the carrying out of repairs as the provision of adequate protection on the line. Special representations on this point have been made to the Minister for Defence, who will do everything possible to facilitate the resumption of traffic'.

Thursday 19. Military authorities request the CB&SC company to run trains to Bantry immediately. Services will recommence tomorrow. Owing to military operations the large number of Irregulars in Sligo area have broken up, and 50 have crossed to Newport via Easkey. Further information received states that the Irregulars have split into columns of 25 under Michael Kilroy and Christy Madden. [In September 1922 Kilroy had been appointed O/C of a new Western Command of the Irregulars; Macken was the leader of a column].

Concern is expressed in the Dáil over the situation on the Dundalk Newry & Greenore. Thomas Johnson (Co. Dublin) says he has been told that the sailings from Greenore have recently been reduced, 'and that everything points to an attempt on the part of the London & North Western Railway Co., as it now is [the line, in fact, has passed into the ownership of the newly-formed London Midland & Scottish] in association with other railways in the north-east corner, to divert traffic through Belfast for the benefit of the British railway connections. I ask that the Ministry will take serious notice of this movement, and let the country know at the earliest possible date what their decisions are in regard to railway policy in general'. Peter Hughes (Louth & Meath) says that he wishes to associate himself with this demand: 'I know from information I have received that what Deputy Johnson has stated is an absolute fact. In fact I would go further, and say that an attempt is being made to boycott the port of Greenore and the port of Dundalk for the betterment of Belfast. I have no hesitation in saying here that the attempt has the sanction of the Great Northern Railway Company and other companies in the North.' Cathal O'Shannon (Louth & Meath) agrees: 'some of us have reason to believe that, if there have not been conversations, there have been what amounted to conversations between certain Northern ministers and certain people connected with the Great Northern Railway for the benefit of areas not inside the Saorstát'. J. B. Whelehan, for the Minister for Industry & Commerce, replies that 'it is not quite correct' that the Dundalk Newry & Greenore is not endeavouring to re-open the line. 'This company has been in communication with the Ministry, and we have made representation to the Minister for Defence that the line from Dundalk to Greenore shall be protected. We are assured that this protection will be immediately forthcoming.' He adds that the Minister for Defence has intimated that on a demand being made by any railway company for protection in any particular area he will take immediate steps to afford it. On the broader issue of traffic poached it was, he suggests, 'an old question, and I think I might just state that at a conference which we had with the railway companies' representatives three or four weeks ago it was intimated to the representatives of the North of Ireland companies that we could not tolerate any artificial means being adopted by those railway companies to promote the interest of ports outside the Saorstát as against ports within it'.

Friday 20. W. T. Cosgrave, President of the Executive Council, suggests to the GNR that the General Manager should investigate and report on the suggestion that the Company absorb those railway systems which cross the Border. These would include the Sligo Leitrim & Northern Counties, the County Donegal, the Londonderry & Lough Swilly and the Dundalk Newry & Greenore.

To meet the Government's request J. F. Sides, Chief Engineer, GS&WR, says he may restart Lisduff quarry provided that satisfactory arrangements can be made for explosives for at least three months. [See 7 March]. [Lisduff, Co. Laois, remains Iarnród Éireann's principal ballast quarry as at 2006].

The MGWR Mayo–Dublin Mail due at Ballymoe at 15.57 is 4 hrs 14 mins late on arrival at Mullingar. The stationmaster at Athlone reports that a goods train travelling to Claremorris was held up by nine armed men. The driver and fireman were ordered off the engine, no. 79 *Mayo*, which was sent at full speed in the direction of Ballymoe station. The Limited Mail with a large number of passengers was waiting there to cross the goods [the line was, and is, single with passing places]. The approaching runaway engine, partly ablaze, was observed by station staff and the driver and fireman of the Mail ran along the track to meet it. The locomotive was slowing for want of steam and the two men succeeded in jumping on and bringing it to a standstill. The goods train was burned and several wagons carrying foodstuffs cleared of their contents. The line is completely blocked and all traffic halted.

Saturday 21. An anonymous correspondent writes in *An t-Óglách, The Irish Army Quarterly*: 'While I was talking to Major-General Russell, in his office at Griffith Barracks, on a sunny Saturday morning about a fortnight ago, we heard the unmistakable sound of a land mine exploding somewhere in the city. Later we learned that an empty carriage on the D&SE line had been blown to smithereens. That was all.' Summarising the function of the Corps the article continues: 'At the present time there are Commands at the following places: Claremorris, Mullingar, Drogheda, Dublin City, Dublin County, Clonmel, Limerick and Cork, and they are just putting out a new Command to be known as the Killarney Command...A Commandant is in charge of the internal organisation of every Command. Each Company in a Command is in charge of a Captain, and each post in the groups of posts is commanded either by a lieutenant or a second lieutenant. The officers themselves live in the blockhouses on the line.The present system of protecting the railways may be stated in order thus: First, Blockhouses; Second, Lancia cars on the tracks. Third, armoured trains; Fourth, patrols between the blockhouses. In particularly bad sections trains are piloted through. The railway companies' traffic is controlled at present from the HQ of the Corps. At Griffith Barracks they know every train that is running, and arrange their plans accordingly. The Companies, in fact, prepare their service timetables in consultation with the Corps. The men are divided into two classes. Class One consists of the technical side of the Corps – railwaymen and others with special training. They are paid at the flat rate of £2 10s per week, without separation or other allowance. Of this amount, however, they received each week only £1. The balance they must either allot to their people or place to their credit... Class Two are paid according to the ordinary Army rates and separation allowance is paid by the Army authorities...'

Armoured train no. 1, Bandon Command, is patrolling the CB&SCR line from Cork to Clonakilty while no. 2 patrols Drimoleague–Bandon. An escort is placed on all trains. The Cork Blackrock & Passage terminus at Albert Street is taken over by Corps troops.

Monday 23. Clonmel Command of the Railway Corps reports that on the 19th last the armoured train proceeded to Limerick and brought back the 25 ton crane for use in the Command. A patrol from the post at Fiddown operating with infantry raided the house of a man named John Connors on night of 19/20th. Connors admitted having assisted in the destruction of railway bridges but stated he was forced to do so by Irregulars who threatened to shoot him if he refused. Connors is also reported as having collected Dog Tax for the Irregulars in the neighbourhood of Fiddown.

Limerick Command states that during the week ending 22 April it placed a Lancia car on patrol duty between Limerick Junction and Two Pot House on the main line and on the Charleville branch. The armoured train conveyed a breakdown gang on clearing operations at Foynes. Troops were escorted from Nenagh to Limerick and the Corps was on escort duty with passengers between the same points. The Nenagh branch was patrolled nightly and an armed escort was provided on all trains on this branch. [The Charleville branch, connecting that town on the main Dublin–Cork line with Patrickswell, junction for Limerick, was opened in 1862 by the Cork & Limerick Direct Railway. Passenger services ceased in 1934 and it was closed completely in 1967].

Tuesday 24. D&SER staff currently under arrest include: Loco Dept. 18 men; Traffic 16; Permanent Way 2. Damage to rolling stock from the commencement of disturbances to 21 April totals: two engines completely destroyed, 12 seriously damaged, six slightly damaged; 17 carriages completely destroyed, 12 seriously damaged, 33 slightly damaged; 24 wagons completely destroyed,

42 seriously damaged, 4 slightly damaged. The General Manager reports that the armoured train was fitted up at the Factory [Grand Canal Street] but that immediately it was completed it was commandeered by the military, notwithstanding his protests, for use on the Killarney branch of the GS&WR Co.

The Wexford–Dublin Mail encounters a large fall of rock at the entrance to the last tunnel before Bray, Co. Wicklow. The driver, Chas. O'Neill, succeeds in reducing speed before the impact and only the loco and the first two coaches leave the rails. There are no casualties.

Claremorris Command of the Railway Protection Corps reports an Irregular GHQ at Aghagower, 5 km from Westport. The school house at Islandeady village (3 km from the station) is being used for meetings by the Irregular leader Mark Killilea.

Wednesday 25. The GS&WR receives a letter from the Ministry of Industry & Commerce with reference to 'the provision of protection for the resumption of railway services at present discontinued owing to the state of the country'. Application is to be made for such protection and suitable arrangements put in place to carry out the work.

At 02.00 three or four armed men hold up Carter and Kerby, two loco men working in the Waterford D&SER loco shed at Newrath on two engines. Having smashed the telephone they return and lock the two men in the shed, stating that they will release them in a short time. The engines are driven down the line towards Waterford station. After an hour and a half one of the engines comes back and stops on touching the door of the shed; the other is found a few yards down the line. The O/C, Waterford, understands that brakes on the tender were not released while the Irregulars were manoeuvring the engines.

Sections closed since July 1922 and remaining closed include Dungarvan–Castletownroche on the GS&WR Waterford–Mallow line; Fermoy–Mitchelstown; Rathmore–Headford Junction–Kenmare; Caragh Lake–Valentia Harbour [then the most westerly railhead in Europe]; Bagenalstown–Palace East; the GS&WR Claremorris–Sligo line; Campile–Killinick–Rosslare; Cobh goods station; and Lisduff quarry works.

In the Dáil, J. B. Whelehan, for the Minister for Industry & Commerce, suggests that 'generally speaking there has been a great improvement within the week in the re-opening of lines of railway'. He provides details:

Dundalk Newry & Greenore. The section between Dundalk and Greenore is closed owing to three bridges being broken thereon. The company has been instructed to apply to the local military authorities for protection and will institute temporary repairs and open the line immediately protection is afforded.

Cork & Macroom Direct. The Ministry is advised that the line will open in three days from the 23rd inst.

Schull & Skibbereen. Entirely closed. The Ministry is advising the company to apply for protection and understands that the damage on the line is not extensive.

Tralee & Dingle. Entirely closed. The Government Consulting Engineer has the question of protection in hands and the Ministry is today advising the company that they should apply to the military authorities. The Minister is informed that the damage to this line can be repaired by the company.

Cork & Muskerry. The line is open for passenger traffic only as Leemount bridge, over which the line runs, is broken. The County Council are repairing this bridge and the Ministry is informed by the General Manager that he expects that the line will be ready for goods traffic in about four weeks.

Cork Blackrock & Passage. Has just been opened for passengers and parcels traffic. Goods service is being maintained by the company's boats on Cork harbour.

Cork Bandon & South Coast. This line is now open as far as Bantry, and Gen. Russell has informed the Ministry that repairs to the Skibbereen branch are in hands. In all the above cases the companies are anxious to resume services and no difficulty will, it is thought, arise.

Great Southern & Western. Closed sections are as listed above. 'The Ministry is in communication with the company regarding protection for these lines, but it is understands that there are some of them which are still badly damaged and there are others on which the company are not anxious to resume a service. The Ministry is, however, pressing them in the matter.'

Listowel & Ballybunion is also entirely closed and the Minister had communicated with the General Manager requesting him to seek the necessary protection. It is understood that the damage to the permanent way has been repaired by the company.

Commenting on the general situation, Mr Whelehan explains that 'the question is what pressure the Minister can bring to bear on the companies. In any case you are up against legal difficulties in the matter...with regard to large bridges, there are large bridges for the repair of which satisfactory arrangements could not be made with the Great Southern & Western Railway, and which are consequently being repaired by the Government'. He goes on to list the bridges affected:

Taylorstown. [Waterford–Rosslare, GS&WR]. Contract let to Hearn's of Waterford. Span and material arriving on site now. [This bridge, no. 457, was destroyed early in July 1922 putting the line out of commission for the duration of the war and for some considerable time afterwards. At the end of 1923 the Cork–Rosslare trains were still travelling via Macmine Junction].

Belvelly. [Cobh Junction (now Glounthane)–Cobh]. Railway Corps erecting a temporary bridge. Contract to be let at once for the provision of a new span.

Monard. [Blarney–Cork on the GS&WR main line]; Carrickabrick [GS&WR Waterford–Rosslare]. Contracts let in both cases to T. J. Moran & Co., Cork. Work in progress.

Dundrum [GS&WR main line Good's Cross–Limerick Junction]. Work well under way, being carried out by Government direct.

Ballyvoile. [GS&WR Waterford–Mallow]. Design submitted by Consulting Engineer approved by railway company. Tenders being invited at the moment. Contract expected to be placed within a week.

Mallow. Work in connection with removal of debris nearing completion. Work in connection with new bridge in full swing in contractor's shop. Men will be on site any day now.

Chetwynd [Cork Bandon & South Coast]. Repairs nearly completed. Practically the whole line now open.

'With regard to road bridges', adds Mr Whelehan, 'all companies are doing repairs except the Great Southern & Western. It is understood that under the Railway Clauses Act the statutory liability for repair rests on the railway company unless excluded by Special Act. The Great Southern & Western Railway, however, states that it has agreements with the County Councils under which the cost of repair is to be born by the Councils. I may say', he concludes, 'the Ministry of Industry & Commerce does bring some compulsion on the railway companies as far as it can, and I should like to say that in the great majority of cases with the exception of the Great Southern & Western Railway Co. we were met half-way in our endeavours to bring about normal traffic.'

Friday 27. The Government Consulting Engineer advises the GS&WR that a contract has been let for timber centring for Monard and Carrig viaducts and that a contract has also been let for the reconstruction of Taylorstown viaduct. He complains that he has received no copies of the drawings or specifications for any of this work. Plans are to be submitted to the next meeting of the board for the rebuilding of stations on the Tullow branch – Grange Con, Dunlavin, Colbinstown, Rathvilly, Tullow. Plans and estimates are to be submitted to the Government Engineer for approval.

Saturday 28. The GNR central signal box at Amiens Street station, Dublin, is maliciously destroyed. The explosion is timed for the moment when an Amiens Street–Drogheda train is passing with some 200 passengers, mostly girls. The blast is accompanied by volleys of rifle and revolver fire from men who have taken up positions on nearby sheds to cover the withdrawal of the mine layers – three youths who had been sitting on a seat on the Howth platform with what appeared to be a brown paper parcel. The military guard, however, observed nothing suspicious and the mine was placed in an aperture under the cabin. When this was done one of the armed youths entered the signal cabin and told signalman McKerr to get out. The side of the cabin is completely blasted out and portions of the masonry hurled through the windows of three or four compartments. 'I was knocked forward in the carriage', says one male passenger, 'and my head hit against the wooden partition separating ours from the next carriage [compartment]. Immediately a shower of bricks and mortar came through the carriage window but somehow or other I escaped being struck, although I suffered badly from the shock of the explosion. In the carriage [compartment] on each side I could hear girls crying and shrieking. They had been cut by the glass which had been shattered and sprayed from the windows.' The Amiens Street signal cabin was the largest in Ireland.

Sunday 29. According to the Government Publicity Department 'railway transport in the Free State is rapidly returning to the normal condition. As far as the trunk lines are concerned the service is practically normal. Visitors to Ireland have no difficulty at present in travelling by rail to almost any portion of the Free State and within the next few weeks it is confidently expected that portions of the country not yet receiving a direct railway service will again be connected with the principal centres'.

'AN ACT OF EXALTED PATRIOTISM'

Tuesday 1. Thousands gather outside Westland Road Station, Dublin, terminus of the D&SER boat trains from Kingstown (now Dun Laoghaire) to welcome the return of Jim Larkin from America, from where he has been deported at his own request following a gaol sentence for membership of the Communist Labor Party and a free pardon by New York Governor Al Smith. At 18.25, at another Dublin terminus, Amiens Street, a D&SER goods tank engine hauling 12 wagons with a consignment of phosphate for Wicklow appears to jump the points outside the station onto a siding and crashes through a wall into the Central Telegraph Office, seriously injuring two telegraphists: Thomas Lombard, 42 Norfolk Rd., Phibsboro and R. J. Roche, 118 Lindsay Rd., Glasnevin. Since the destruction of the signal box [see 28 April] points have had to be worked by hand [see 24 May].

Wednesday 2. The Dáil is told that the railway companies have not so far come to an agreement as to a grouping scheme, but following on discussions which have taken place with the principal companies on the present position it is possible that the further consideration they are now giving to the matter will result in a basis of agreement.

Thursday 3. The MGWR agrees to a scale of charges to be made by the four Dublin railway companies for facilities provided for National Army troops. In respect of the five armoured trains, the actual cost of conversion and cost of subsequent restoration to original state are to be charged. In the case of an armoured train converted by one company and used on that company's system, actual cost of wages and coal, oil and other stores consumed are to be charged. A special charge will apply when the train is converted by one company but used over another company's system. Regarding the use of wagons attached to an armoured train for conveyance of stores and materials there will be no charge where stores, etc. are being conveyed for construction or protection of the company's property; otherwise the ordinary military rate applies.

Friday 4. A communication is received by the GS&WR from the General Post Office requesting that during the continued suspension of the up Night Mail service the 08.45 train ex Mallow which is due at Kingsbridge [now Heuston, Dublin] at 13.30 should be accelerated so as to reach there at 13.00 to enable letters arriving by that train to be included in the last delivery of the day in Dublin. The request will be complied with.

Sunday 6. An armoured train under the command of Colonel Naus, a Belgian serving with the Free State forces, proceeds with a 20-ton crane to Ballinacurra on the Waterford–Limerick line at 09.00 and spends the day working on wrecked trains, removing debris from the smash at Rathcurby bridge. It returns to Clonmel at 17.15. [Subsequently, on 4 June, the armoured train proceeds to Waterford where it requisitions a heavy GS&WR engine and returns with it to Rathcurby, where both engines are coupled together and hitched with a chain to the wrecked engine, no. 211. The latter is pulled out, towed to Waterford and handed over to its owners, the GS&WR].

Wednesday 9. Report from Tralee Command, RPR&MC: 'On the night of the 9th 46194 Sergt. Muldowney, T, NCO i/c Caragh Lake Outpost, whilst under the influence of drink, proceeded with a party to raid the houses in the vicinity of his post. Whilst raiding the Post Office a member of the party, 33413 Pte. McCaffrey, J., through careless handling accidentally discharged his rifle wounding Pte. Byrne in the thighs.'

All five lines radiating from Cork are again in operation, though in some cases with limited service, and there remain only a few coastal centres dependent upon supplies and transport by sea.

Thursday 10. In the Dáil, Michael Hennessy (Cork E & NE) asks the Minister for Industry & Commerce, Joseph McGrath, whether he is aware that the bridge at Fota, Co Cork, is not yet repaired. The Assistant Minister, J. B. Whelehan, replies: 'A contract for the permanent repair of the bridge has already been placed and the work is proceeding. The repair is due for completion by 16 June next.' Mr Hennessy: 'it is now over five weeks since I asked a similar question to this, and was told that the bridge would be repaired within a fortnight from then, but still nothing has been done...' Mr Whelehan: 'The previous answer dealt with temporary repairs to be carried out by the Maintenance Corps.' Mr Hennessy: 'Do I understand from the Minister that the Maintenance Corps are about to re-open this bridge temporarily in the near future, and that we can get communication between Cobh and Cork over this bridge within the next fortnight or three weeks through the medium of the Maintenance Corps?' Mr Whelehan: 'Permanent repairs are to be completed by the 16th of June.' Mr Hennessy: 'That is a long way off.'

Domhnall Ó Ceallacháin (Wexford) asks the Assistant Minister if he will state what steps are being taken to have the Rosslare route re-opened and, if possible, the Great Western Railway boats to resume their sailings [to Fishguard]. Mr Whelehan informs him that it is improbable that there will be sufficient traffic offering to justify a resumption of sailing until the repairs of some of the larger viaducts damaged on the GS&WR's southern lines have further progressed. 'The work', he says, 'has to be undertaken by the Government and is being expedited as much as possible.'

Friday 11. The Great Southern & Western appoint E. C. Bredin Works Manager at a salary of £700 per annum. [He is to become Locomotive Superintendent of the amalgamated Great Southern Railways in 1937 and its General Manager in 1941]. Mountmellick goods store is to be rebuilt at an estimated cost of £1,100 on receipt of compensation. [Mountmellick was reached from a junction at Portlaoise in 1885 by the Central Ireland Railway, which intended to continue its line to Mullingar. This was never achieved, and Mountmellick remained at the end of short and unprofitable branch which was closed to all traffic in 1963]

Saturday 12. Drogheda Command, Railway Protection Corps: 'Message received from Dublin that a wanted Irregular named Butterly was seen entering the slip carriage of the 15.00 train at Amiens Street. On arrival of the train, a man who answered the description given was arrested and handed over to the Infantry at Millmount Barracks.'

It is announced that the Mallow [South]–Killarney service will be restored on Monday and simultaneously Headford–Kenmare and Farranfore–Cahirciveen–Valentia. Maj.-Gen. Russell inspected the Tralee–Dingle line yesterday with the Manager, John P Tooher, and after satisfying himself as to the stability of the repaired bridges has decided to have the line re-opened for traffic on Tuesday next.

Sunday 13. The reconstruction of Belvelly Bridge [Cobh Junction–Cobh] has been completed and a trial test of 500 tons satisfactorily carried out. The Tralee–Dingle line has been re-opened ahead of schedule and posts established at Derry Quay, Camp Junction, Glenmore, Anascaul, Lispole and Dingle. All trains are escorted.

Monday 14. The O/C Limerick Command of the Railway Protection Corps proceeds by armoured train to Leamy's Bridge and removes the entire garrison, as information has been received that many of the men are 'on terms of the greatest intimacy' with the people in the district.

Tuesday 15. The question of bringing the new D&SER engines, nos. 461 and 462, from Belfast for immediate use is deferred until the board meeting on the 29th when the question of the engine stock will be fully considered. The General Manager, J. Coghlan, reports that from 23 April to 14 May there has been only one raid, that being at the parcels office, Foxrock, in which clothing was taken out of a trunk and scattered about the floor. Crowley & Partners, Consulting Engineers for the Government, have approved plans for the renewal of bridges 367, Palace East and 278, Gorey.

The claims of Galway as an international port are urged upon the Minister for Industry & Commerce by a deputation representing Galway Chamber of Commerce, Galway County Council and the Midland Great Western. M F Keogh, General Manager of the latter, says that the railway 'would be able to deal with a very large amount of additional traffic'.

The MGWR receives an application from stationmaster Hogge, Sligo, for an advance to replace such part of his furniture destroyed by fire on 10 January last which he says is essential for his use pending Government compensation. He is granted the sum of £105. 13s. 0d. Clonmel Command of the Railway Protection Corps continues to work on the wreckage at Rathcurby and re-rails the tender of GS&WR 0-6-0 loco no.211, built as an 0-6-2T in 1903 and rebuilt in 1907. [Scrapped in 1959]. The line between Tralee and Valentia, via Farranfore, is re-opened.

Thursday 17. The stationmaster at Donoughmore on the Cork & Muskerry is arrested by the military. He will resume duty on 28 June. The announcement that a provisional agreement for amalgamation has been reached by the directors of the GS&WR and MGWR results in a sharp rise in MGWR stock on the Dublin Exchange. It is expected that the D&SER will also come into the group.

On the Cork & Macroom Direct Railway all trains are now escorted from the Cork terminus at Capwell to Killumney by troops of the Railway Preservation Corps and from Macroom to Killumney by infantry. The Corps is to take over the latter duty in the near future. Engine no 6 of the CB&SCR has been handed over to its Killarney Command which is also utilising engine no. 2, a 4-4-0T with its cab armoured, for patrol duty.

Friday 18. The GS&WR grants bonuses to the manageresses at Parknasilla, Caragh Lake and Kenmare (£20, £15, £15) as an appreciation of the excellent manner in which they remained at their posts in trying circumstances. Daily through services Tuam–Sligo are to be restored from the 19th (passenger) and 21st (goods). The Birdhill–Killaloe service is also to be restored. [This short branch, opened in 1862, was extended to Killaloe pier five years later and saw occasional passenger services in connection with the Shannon river steamers. Passenger services ceased in 1931 and the branch closed completely in 1944].

A letter to the GS&WR from Swinford Rural District Council, Co. Mayo, encloses a copy of a resolution which was adopted by them protesting against the 'unwarrantable delay' in resuming the working of the line from Collooney to Claremorris, closed since last July. The Council is to be informed that the company was only advised two days ago that the line was now safe to work and accordingly will start working it as from tomorrow. An inspection of the Tullow branch is carried out. Harristown signal cabin is burned down; Dunlavin signal cabin is also burned down, and will be rebuilt in concrete. The goods store is fire-damaged and will be repaired. The station building, also burned, will be rebuilt in concrete; At Colbinstown, the signal cabin and station, also burned, will be rebuilt in concrete block, as will be the booking office and waiting shed at Grange Con, also burned. [Séamus de Burca, in 'Growing up in Dublin' (*Dublin Historical Record*, June 1976) recalled: 'The Civil War had started when my father took Kevin and me to spend the summer in Killelan. We got out of the train at Baltinglass, although the local station was Grangecon. Baltinglass was occupied by Irregular forces. Their troops were in the station, watching the arrival of the train...'] The Rathvilly signal cabin and station buildings are burnt and will be restored; Tullow, signal cabin is burned down, the booking office and former telegraph office fire-damaged. These will be restored, but a decision on the loading bank has been postponed.

Killorglin–Valentia is not, in fact, yet re-opened: the revised date is Monday 28.

Sunday 20. At 03.00 the stationmaster at Foxrock, Co. Dublin, is compelled by two unknown men to open the booking office out of which the raiders take an amount of £2. 15s. 8d. and 12 detonators. The General Manager of the D&SER is requested to call the attention of the Civic Guard to the frequent raids made on this station and to request suitable protection of the premises.

Wednesday 23. The CB&SCR line between Drimoleague and Skibbereen is reopened. Claremorris Command of the Railway Protection Corps reports that general Irregular activity has resumed in the Curry–Leyney area and that the Irregular leader Patrick McCarthy is again getting men together. The reported strength of the column is 42. Cork Command returns armoured cab engine no. 2 to the owners who will hold it in reserve, while Claremorris Command troops from Tubbercurry and Curry, in co-operation with infantry, capture three Irregulars, Nelson, McLoughlin and Duffy, the last named Frank Carty's Brigade Quartermaster. Carty had used a Volunteer posing as a priest and successfully seized 30 rifles, one machine gun, some revolvers and ammunition in Tubbercurry. The armoured train is working between Curry and Collooney in operations against Carty's column.

Thursday 24. The end of the War. [see Tuesday 29]. Recent escorts for trains to and from Valentia were for special private trains, which have now been discontinued. The line is not yet open to ordinary traffic.

In an enquiry into the 1 May accident at Amiens Street station Thomas Batchen, Ministry of

Industry & Commerce, finds that pilotman James MacDonald was at fault in not seeing for himself, before he went out to Newcomen to pilot the train to the station, that the points were properly made for no. 4 road instead of remaining fixed for the turntable.

Friday 25. The Bandon Command armoured train no. 2 is patrolling between Bantry and Bandon on the CB&SCR. Belvelly Bridge on the Cork–Cobh line is now open to traffic. J. M. Savage, stationmaster, GS&WR Waterford Coaching, receives a notification from the IRA that as he was instructed to leave the country previously and has returned without authority he should leave Ireland again within 24 hours after receipt of this notice. The military authorities have now made satisfactory arrangements for the supply of explosives to Lisduff quarry, which is to re-open on 27 May.

Saturday 26. With an expected increase in tourist traffic in view of the prospects for peace now prevailing the railway companies are planning to introduce cheaper fares to holiday destinations as from 1 June. The Mullingar Command posts at Kilgarvan and Blattery Bridge have withdrawn.

Monday 28. In the Dáil, Riobard Ó Deaghaidh [Robert Day] (Cork) asks the Minister for Defence 'whether his is aware that a soldier named Hogan, who prior to his enlistment was a railway signalman and is on duty as a soldier for 16 hours per day whereas his duty as a railway signalman did not exceed eight hours per day and whether this action has given rise to considerable dissatisfaction to the local railwaymen, and whether he will issue instructions to have this man set to his ordinary duty immediately'. General Mulcahy: 'I am not aware that Hogan is on duty for 16 hours a day. He was for short periods owing to a difficulty experienced by the railway company concerned in getting signalmen capable of operating a certain cabin. I am also not aware that there has been any dissatisfaction among local signalmen arising out of Hogan's duties. It is now possible to release Hogan from military service, and he is being returned to his ordinary duty forthwith.'

Tuesday 29. A north to northeast wind carries a hint of frost. According to the front page of the *Cork Examiner* Mr de Valera, in a message addressed to the soldiers of Liberty, Legion of the Rearguard, declares the Republic can no longer successfully be defended by arms, and describes the laying aside of arms as 'an act of exalted patriotism'...Mr Frank Aiken, Chief of Staff [Irregulars], states that arms are to be dumped: 'The foreign and domestic enemies of the Republic have for the moment prevailed'. On the same page, and equally belatedly, T.A. Sheedy & Co. Ltd. of Commercial Building, 77 South Mall, advertise 'RIOT AND CIVIL COMMOTION INSURANCE ON MOTORS – we are now able to effect Policies to cover the above risks...' Elsewhere the war continues, Drogheda Command of the Railway Protection Corps reporting that the infantry post at Gullsville station has been heavily attacked for three hours. 'In view of the attack O/C Command does not propose withdrawing any Posts for the present.'

The weekly board meeting of the D&SER is informed that no raid accompanied by pillage has occurred since 29 April. A consignment described as bicarbonate of soda from Belfast, a material used in the manufacture of high explosive, is in hands at New Ross and has been taken over by the CID. In the matter of the armoured train, the question of the return of the engine and the special payment for the use of the train is referred to the General Purposes Committee. The General Manager is authorised to have the two new engines, 2-6-os nos. 461 and 462, returned from Belfast, where they have been stabled in the GNR's Adelaide Depot, and brought into use. He and Mr Wild are requested to see that they are used 'discreetly' for some time to come. [One of them, no. 461, will survive the end of steam and pass into the care of the Railway Preservation Society of Ireland]. Fireman Hammond, who was arrested on 7 March, has been released by the Government having signed the prescribed undertaking and is again at work, though forfeiting his pay while under arrest.

Wednesday 30. The RPR&MC Claremorris Command reports one prisoner named Gannon arrested in the Tubbercurry-Curry area, and that two poitín stills were discovered during the same operations.

Thursday 31. Further withdrawal of Mullingar Command. Posts: from Thomastown (Athlone–Galway) and Kiltoom (Athlone–Claremorris); Thurles Command: Posts at Ballindine,

EPILOGUE

I NCIDENTS OCCURRED SPORADICALLY into June and July, but for the railways it was effectively over. In early June they reached agreement with the Minister for Finance in the matter of the Damage to Property (Compensations) Act 1923 through which the Government was make good a proportion at least of the extensive losses ranging from the complete destruction of property to £900 worth of articles taken by the Irregulars from the Great Southern & Western's hotel at Parknasilla: it was decided that for the present these were not to be replaced though it was planned to re-open the hotel on 12 July 1923. The railway hotels, significant contributors to the companies' balance sheet, had suffered severely during the war. On 8 June the GS&WR's Chief Civil Engineer, John F. Sides, was instructed to call on the Government Consulting Engineer, Dr Crowley, to ascertain which over-bridges the Government wanted renewed first, and to proceed on those lines. In many cases the estimates furnished by the company were not accepted in full by the Government: the former estimated the cost of rebuilding Grange station at £908 5s 8d but was offered only £899 8s 8d – the offer was accepted.

On 22 June the GS&WR board was informed that the Free State Army Council were pressing the railways for reduced fare facilities for the conveyance of troops similar to those given to the British army prior to Control. The company, however, decided that it had suffered more than any other in Ireland and that it was impossible to envisage any reduction in fares at that time. The estimated cost of making good the damage to rolling stock, etc. up to 23 May 1923 amounted to £123,827, against which the Chief Mechanical Engineer, J. R. Bazin, has spent, up to the same period, £30,630 in making good some of the damage. In addition £47,083 had been spent on armouring cars, and on engine power for armoured trains but, complained Bazin, the Government had only paid on account some £34, 579.

There was an incident on Sunday 8 July when a GS&WR special carrying 279 passengers returning from Listowel to Castleisland, Co. Kerry, ran over an iron gate which has been placed on the line, but damage was slight. Though some of their patrols, particularly in the south-west, were still operating, by this time a high proportion of the Railway Protection Corps' posts had been withdrawn. On 18 June, however, an armoured train had patrolled the Nenagh branch previous to the arrival of President Cosgrave from Dublin. He inspected the positions at Nenagh, Birdhill and Castleconnell and expressed his appreciation of the smart appearance of the men. Fifty Other Ranks formed a guard of honour on his arrival at Limerick station. By 21 July 153 officers and 3095 other ranks had been transferred to the Special Infantry or demobilised: the Corps had served its purpose. One of its last acts was to open a 'concentration camp' (the term was yet to acquire its sinister connotation) at Fota, to which the Cork Command HQ was transferred in early July.

As the dust died down it was clear that the major questions concerning the future of the railways remained to be answered. In January 1923 Cosgrave had told the Dáil that early the previous month it had become apparent that there was likely to be a disagreement between the parties as the year drew to an end and that representatives of the companies had been invited to meet the Government to discuss the position. There were, he said, two new factors then to be considered which altered essentially the nature of the railways problem as far as the Government was concerned. Firstly, the implications of the reports of the Railway Commission and secondly the fact that the destruction which the railways had suffered had seriously prejudiced the financial position of some of the companies.

The Commission had issued two reports. The Majority Report recommended a system of State ownership, with management not by the State, but by a body representing the users of the railways, the trade unions and the Minister for Finance. The Minority Report recommended unification under the management of a similar body, with the addition of representation of the shareholders and a guarantee by the State to the shareholders of dividends on the basis received in 1921, which was practically the same as 1913, the most profitable year in the history of the railway concerns. 'The Government found itself unable to accept either report', said Cosgrave: 'if the State is to purchase the railways the State must retain control over the management and expenditure, and a Minister must be answerable to the Dáil for all branches of administration. The Government is not in favour of this policy, and it is indeed condemned by the Majority Report itself, which has little faith in the capacity of a Government Department to manage the railway system...In any case, purchase by the State would involve a financial operation which both reports recognise would be embarrassing to the State at the present time.'

Having been informed of the Government's position in December 1922 the main railways were seriously considering a grouping scheme, but the D&SER flatly refused to have anything to do with the GS&WR, fearing, with some justification, that it would be swallowed up by the larger concern. On 7 June 1923, however, the Board of the Cork Bandon & South Coast decided to join the new organisation as proposed by Sir William Goulding, the powerful chairman of the GS&WR, and under the threat of legislation to enforce a grouping system an agreement was reached, though the political division of the country meant that the Great Northern and the smaller cross-border lines had to be left out of the equation. The Railways Act of 1924, therefore, brought together in the Great Southern Railway the companies in the Free State with the exception of the Listowel & Ballybunion, virtually destroyed in the war and considered both an operational and financial embarrassment.

On 4 October 1923 the new GS&WR 4-6-0 loco no. 405 drew the first train, carrying the President of the Executive Council, across the restored Mallow viaduct. Before the crossing 'the President left his compartment', according to the *Cork Examiner*, 'while a party of national soldiers drawn up on the railway track came to the salute, and walked with Sir William Goulding to the engine'. The train passed over the new bridge, severing the tricolour ribbons that had been stretched across the track. The symbolism was apparent: for the railways, the closing of the rift between 'Mallow North' and 'Mallow South' signalling that, for them, the war was well and truly over. The more debilitating rift in the national psyche would be a matter for another day.

SELECT BIBLIOGRAPHY

Primary Sources

Board and other minutes of the principal railway companies held in the CIÉ Archive, Heuston Station, Dublin.

Collins, Seán M., *Civil War in Drogheda*. Unpublished MA thesis, UCD 1999.

Dáil Reports Vols. 1-3, 1922-3.

Material relating to the Railway Protection, Repair & Maintenance Corps held in the Military Archives, Cathal Brugha Barracks, Dublin.

Young, Mrs Esmay, Dundalk. Personal correspondence, courtesy of Canice O'Mahony, grandson.

Secondary Sources

BOOKS

Andrews, C.S., *Dublin Made Me* (Dublin & Cork, 1979)

Barrington, T., *Discovering Kerry* (Dublin, 1976)

Baker, Michael H.C., *Irish Railways since 1916* (London, 1972)

Beaumont, Jonathan, *Rails to Achill* (Usk, 2002)

Casserley, H.C., *Outline of Irish Railway History* (Newton Abbot, 1974)

Coogan, T.P & George Morrison, *The Irish Civil War* (London, 1998)

Corcoran, Michael, *Through Streets Broad and Narrow* (Leicester, 2000)

Duggan, John P., *A History of the Irish Army* (Dublin, 1991)

Flanagan, Patrick J., *The Cavan & Leitrim Railway* (London, 1972)

Hamilton, J.A.B., *Britain's Railways in World War 1* (London, 1967)

Harrington, Niall C., *Kerry Landing* (Dublin, 1992)

Hopkinson, Michael. *Green Against Green*. Dublin 2004.

Johnson, Stephen, *Johnson's Atlas & Gazetteer of the Railways of Ireland* (Leicester, 1997)

Mac Aongusa, Brian, *Broken Rails. Crashes and Sabotage on Irish Railways* (Dublin, 2005)

McNeill, D.B., *Irish Passenger Steamship Services Vol. 2: South of Ireland* (Newton Abbot, 1971)

Maybin, J.M., *Belfast Corporation Tramways 1905-1954* (Broxbourne)

Morrison, George, *The Irish Civil War* (Dublin, 1981)

Murphy, Jeremiah, *When Youth was Mine*. Dublin 1998.

Murray, K.A.&D.B., McNeill, *The Great Southern & Western Railway* (Dublin 1978)

Newham, A.T., *The Cork & Muskerry Light Railway* (Lingfield, 1968)

—*The Schull and Skibbereen Tramway* (Lingfield, 1964)

O'Farrell, Padraig, *Who's Who in the War of Independence & Civil War 1916-1923* (Dublin, 1997)

O'Neill. Jack, *Engines and Men* (Portlaw, 2005)

—*Waterford – a History* (Waterford, 1992)

Pryce, Irwin & Leslie McAlister, *Steaming in Three Centuries* (London, 2006)

Rowledge, J.W.P., *A Regional History of Railways. Volume 16 Ireland* (Penryn, 1995)

Shepherd, E., *The Dublin & South Eastern Railway* (Newton Abbot, 1974)

—*The Midland Great Western Railway of Ireland* (Leicester, 1994)

Younger, C., *Ireland's Civil War* (London, 1968)

NEWSPAPERS & PERIODICALS

Anon, 'The Railway protection, Repair and Maintenance Corps', *An t-Óglách*, Dublin 21 April 1923

Bergin, W.J., 'Ambush on the Grey Ghost', *An Cosantóir*, Vol. 38, 5 (Dublin, May 1978)

Coyne, Edward J., 'The Railway Problem', *Studies Vol. XII* (Dublin, 1923)

Harden, G., 'The War on the Railways in Wexford', *Journal of the Irish Railway Record Society, Vol. III, 12, 13* (Dublin, 1953)

McGrath, Walter, 'The Fenians at Rathduff', *Journal of the Irish Railway Record Society, Vol. 9, no. 50* (Dublin, 1969/70)

Rowlands, David & Walter McGrath, 'The Dingle Train in the Life of Corkaguiny.' *Journal of the Kerry Archaeological and Historical Society, No.11* (Tralee, 1978)

White, M. 'Fifty Years of a Loco Man's Life.' *Journal of the Irish Railway Record Society, Vol. 6, 3* (Dublin 1963)

Cork Examiner, Irish Independent, Tuam Herald, Waterford News etc., 1922–3

Journal of the Irish Railway Record Society, Dublin. *Passim*

INDEX